THE HAMMERS
OF CREATION

THE HAMMERS
OF CREATION

Folk Culture
in Modern
African-American
Fiction

Eric J. Sundquist

Mercer University

Lamar Memorial Lectures No. 35

The University of Georgia Press

Athens and London

© 1992 by the University of Georgia Press
Athens, Georgia 30602
All rights reserved
Designed by Betty Palmer McDaniel
Set in 10/14 ITC Cheltenham Light by
Tseng Information Systems, Inc.
Printed and bound by Maple-Vail Book Manufacturing Group
The paper in this book meets the guidelines for
permanence and durability of the Committee on
Production Guidelines for Book Longevity of the
Council on Library Resources.

Printed in the United States of America

96   95   94   93   92   C   5   4   3   2   1

Library of Congress Cataloging in Publication Data
Sundquist, Eric J.
The hammers of creation : folk culture in modern
African-American fiction / Eric J. Sundquist.
p.   cm. — (Mercer University Lamar memorial lectures ;
no. 35)
Includes bibliographical references and index.
ISBN 0-8203-1460-9 (alk. paper)
1. American fiction—Afro-American authors—History and
criticism.   2. Johnson, James Weldon, 1871–1938.
Autobiography of an ex-coloured man.   3. Bontemps, Arna
Wendell, 1902–1973. Black thunder.   4. Hurston, Zora
Neale. Jonah's gourd vine.   5. Literature and folklore—
United States.   6. Afro-Americans in literature.   7. Afro-
Americans—Folklore.   8. Folklore in literature.   I. Title.
II. Series: Lamar memorial lectures ; no. 35.
PS374.N4S87   1992
813.009'3520396073—dc20   91–46523
CIP

British Library Cataloging in Publication Data available

for
Alexandra, Joanna, and Ariane

CONTENTS

FOREWORD

In October 1991, Mercer University was privileged to have as the thirty-fifth lecturer in its Lamar Memorial Lecture Series one of the leading literature scholars and intellectual historians in America. Born and raised in a Kansas town named for a Union general, and having spent his teaching career in faraway California, Eric J. Sundquist has nonetheless established himself as a perceptive commentator on southern history. To those who attended his lectures, the brilliance of his presentation demonstrated conclusively his broad knowledge and deep understanding of the culture of the South.

And many people attended. Despite stiff competition from the World Series—which, in addition to a team from the far North, featured the pride of Georgia, the nearby Atlanta Braves—Professor Sundquist spoke to overflow audiences.

What he told his auditors, presented here in a format not bound by time constraints, dealt with important matters in the experience of black southerners. The rich contextuality of *The Hammers of Creation* establishes beyond question the significance of fiction by three black southern writers that has too often been neglected. Professor Sundquist's analysis of James Weldon Johnson's study of music, Zora Neale Hurston's exploration of folklore, and Arna Bontemps's examination of history enhances not only our knowledge of black folk culture but also our understanding of the complex relationship of black and white life in the South.

The bequest of Eugenia Dorothy Blount Lamar, which endowed this series, stipulated that the lectures exemplify "the very highest type of scholarship" and that they "aid in the permanent preservation of the values of southern culture, history, and literature." *The Hammers of Creation* admirably fulfills Mrs. Lamar's vision.

Wayne Mixon
for the Lamar Memorial
Lectures Committee

PREFACE

As extended versions of the 1991 Lamar Memorial Lectures, the chapters that follow bear some marks of the less formal style that a speaking format allows. Because they contain relatively few direct quotations, even from the primary literary texts by James Weldon Johnson, Zora Neale Hurston, and Arna Bontemps, I have elected to forego annotation and have instead provided a bibliography of works cited and of other major studies that bear closely on the topic of African-American folklore in its relation to literature. I have chosen the phrase "folk culture" in my subtitle, but I might also have used "vernacular culture" or even "slave culture," insofar as the former points to the tradition of oral narrative, or vocal expression, that is central to my interpretations, and the latter has come to embrace a positive range of cultural forms nurtured in slavery while also reflecting African traditions that were carried forward in important instances of postemancipation culture and modern black literature. The main title, *The Hammers of Creation*, is borrowed from the sermon by the Reverend C. C. Lovelace that was first transcribed, set into verse form, and published by Zora Neale Hurston in a 1934 essay before being cast into her novel *Jonah's Gourd Vine*. The phrase has a range of evocative implications, the most specific explored in chapter 2, yoking the labor of African Americans to their spiritual beliefs and pointing to the manner in which each of the authors I treat celebrates the centrality of black folk life in the artistic endeavor.

The studies in this volume are to some degree a continuation of my interpretations of the role of race in American culture pursued at length in *To Wake the Nations: Race in American Literature and Culture, 1830–1930*. In *To Wake the Nations*, evaluations of the importance of African-American folktales, spirituals, and vernacular culture to the work of Charles Chesnutt and W. E. B. Du Bois in particular (and in different ways, the autobiographical texts of Frederick Douglass and the recorded "Confessions" of Nat Turner) led me to seek fresh ways to recontextualize their major writings as part of a larger tradition in African-American culture and American literary history generally. To the extent that Johnson, Hurston, and Bontemps in distinct but overlapping ways continue the kind of multi-dimensional work in which Chesnutt and Du Bois engaged, *The Hammers of Creation* is an extension of the longer critical study—from which a few short passages have been reworked to illuminate the novels at hand—and may therefore be read in light of its more complete annotation.

Nevertheless, these chapters would likely have no separate existence but for the generous invitation to deliver the 1991 Lamar Lectures at Mercer University. I want to thank the Lamar Memorial Lectures Committee and the faculty of Mercer for their most cordial reception and the exciting intellectual forum provided by the occasion of the lectures. Most of all, let me especially thank Fran and Wayne Mixon, both for their years of friendship and for their kind hospitality during my visit. As on many other occasions, Wayne has also given me his excellent advice about various aspects of this book. A few other acknowledgments are also in order. Although they may have forgotten it, two of my 1989 colleagues at the Bread Loaf School of English, Professor Dixie Goswami of Clemson University and Mr. Michael Obel-omia, offered me views of the vernacular elements in *Black Thunder* that have been instrumental in my thinking about that book and others. The lecture on Bontemps was also improved by responses to it from audiences at the University of Kansas, Kansas State University, and Vanderbilt University; and graduate students in a UCLA seminar on southern fiction sharpened my understanding of all three novels.

of the vernacular elements in *Black Thunder* that have been instrumental in my thinking about that book and others. The lecture on Bontemps was also improved by responses to it from audiences at the University of Kansas, Kansas State University, and Vanderbilt University; and graduate students in a UCLA seminar on southern fiction sharpened my understanding of all three novels.

THE HAMMERS

OF CREATION

ONE

"These Old Slave Songs": *The Autobiography of an Ex-Coloured Man*

In the moment of crisis near the conclusion of James Weldon Johnson's masterful critique of Jim Crow, when the anonymous narrator, confronted with a southern lynching, decides at last to forsake his African-American racial inheritance, go north, and pass for white, perhaps nothing is stranger than the narrative tone. Take the example of this prosaic passage, in which the protagonist describes the black spirituals he has heard in rural Georgia: "As yet, the Negroes themselves do not fully appreciate these old slave songs. The educated classes are rather ashamed of them and prefer to sing hymns from books. This feeling is natural; they are still too close to the conditions under which the songs were produced; but the day will come when this slave music will be the most treasured heritage of the American Negro." On the face of it, this is an unremarkable passage. It describes an opinion about slave culture that was commonplace at the turn of the century, and the only peculiarity lies in the fact that it sounds like an extract from an editorial rather than a novel. Today, the centrality of the black spirituals to American culture is taken for granted,

but when Johnson was writing there would still have been considerable dissent from an argument in favor of the spirituals; the
flourishing ethnological debate frequently circled around the re-
luctance of postslavery generations to value and preserve black
antebellum music, let alone sing it in the "authentic" style. Johnson himself would later make arguments similar to this passage in
his prefaces to the first *Book of American Negro Spirituals* (1925)
and the *Book of American Negro Poetry* (1922), and the narrator's opinion, like other such passages in the novel that were to
be echoed in Johnson's nonfiction, does not at first glance seem
worth particular attention.

And yet, there is significant disequilibrium in the narrator's remark about "these old slave songs" when it is placed in the context
of the novel. To begin with, who are "the Negroes themselves" that
this passage identifies? The whole burden of the climactic chapter 10, in which this observation is couched, is to demonstrate that
the narrator, already hiding behind his cloak of light skin even before he makes his final renunciation of blackness, identifies with
few if any "Negroes"—certainly not with the equally anonymous
lynching victim, his dark double, with whom he is about to be confronted, nor with those rural folk who do appreciate and continue
the tradition of the old slave songs, the black Georgians whose
culture becomes the crucible of his own hypocritical "shame at
being identified with a people that could with impunity be treated
worse than animals." The chapter shows, moreover, that those
who disdain the spirituals are *not* those who are "still too close"
to the conditions of slavery but rather the postemancipation generation, those who hope they have escaped the stigma of slavery
or who aspire to white middle-class values or who, like Johnson
himself in his preface to the second *Book of American Negro Spirituals* (1926), argued that the spirituals could be best preserved
and honored by modulation into the music of high—that is, Euro-

pean—culture: "Why cannot this nobler music of the Negro in the hands of our serious composers be wrought into the greater American music that has so long been looked for?"

The cultural passage from slavery to post-Reconstruction necessitated such an argument even as it exacted the costs that *The Autobiography of an Ex-Coloured Man* (1912) records, for in singing "hymns from books" or arranging the spirituals into more regular, predictable concertized forms, the next generation risked losing the spontaneity, passion, and African inflections of a magnificent vernacular art. Into the chronological slippage between the old slave generations truly "close to the conditions under which the songs were produced" and Johnson's generation, many of whom had a "natural" aversion to the remnants of slave culture, the narrative inserts the most heavily encoded, ritually complex "passage"—a passage in which the extremities of Jim Crow, the longing to re-create and remember African-American origins, and the apparently futile desire to break down the American color barrier are set in conflict.

The stated disdain of some blacks for "these old slave songs" was widespread enough in post-Reconstruction years to be blithely labeled "natural" by Johnson's protagonist. But like "shame," the "natural" in this novel is a category under continual pressure, containing in miniature the ethical and epistemological burdens of the race question as it was being adjudicated in scientific, sociological, and legal arenas in which an appeal to the ambiguous "laws of nature" was time and again cited as a justification, or at least an explanation, for segregation and racial violence. The appeal to nature in this deceptively expository passage requires that we think of other such instances in the protagonist's self-serving narrative—for instance, his claim that "the fact that the whites of the South despise and ill-treat the desperate [lower] class of blacks is . . . explainable according to the ancient laws of human nature," or the narrator's more radically disjunctive assertion at the novel's end that he constantly feared his white wife "would unconsciously attribute" some shortcoming in his character to his "blood rather than to a failing of human nature." Such passages adumbrate broad moral issues of the novel, but they serve as well to reiterate how complex is the seemingly simplest prose of *The Autobiography of an Ex-Coloured Man*, in which fictive autobiographical narrative, cultural essay, historical allegory, and signifying parody are intertwined.

Riddled with epistemological obscurities and moral evasions that define the anonymous narrator's inconclusive escape from his own racial heritage, Johnson's text is an improvisatory act of remarkable subtlety and flare. His original intention to entitle his novel *The Chameleon* was an apt reflection not only of the narrator's changing identity—the variable refractions of his ambiguous "color"—but more so of his (and Johnson's) risky cultural project. The entire novel participates in the work of historical recovery, the shaping and saving of memory, in which African Americans were especially engaged as slave culture threatened to fade from view by virtue of both the passing of the slave generations and the rising severities of Jim Crow. Johnson at once underscored the value of such historical recovery and subjected the acts of recollection and cultural recovery to merciless scrutiny. By searching the dimensions of his protagonist's own "dual personality," a concept elaborated in literal terms from Du Bois's famous dictum about American racial doubleness in *The Souls of Black Folk* (1903), Johnson addressed a crisis that was at once legal, psychological, and historical.

Narrated in retrospect by a canny storyteller who chooses to pass into a culture of privilege and power rather than face the difficulty of being black in a world of segregation, *The Autobiography of an Ex-Coloured Man* is also about "passing" in several other senses as well—the passing of slave culture, the manifold geographical passages that have defined African-American life from its beginnings, and the passing of vernacular culture into the transfigured, assimilated idioms of so-called high culture. All these connotations of passing are melded together in the book's constant passing of narrative authority between the smug, calculating narrator and Johnson himself, who, as his later essay "The Dilemma of the Negro Author" (1928) would make clear, was acutely aware that the black writer was constrained in his subject matter by both sides of the color line: he could not choose white subjects; he must not embarrass African Americans by choosing certain delicate black subjects; and he was hard pressed to avoid capitulation to the popular stereotypes of minstrelsy. Johnson did not write his own autobiography, of course, but he did write his own and his culture's spiritual autobiography at a moment of particular historical tension and risk. Cloaked in an experimental anonymity that was crucial to his book's great achievement but which also gave him the license necessary to dissect early modern black culture as it was formed in the age of segregation, Johnson is neither synonymous with his narrator nor entirely separable from him. Rather, the equivocal language of his novel depicts him constantly passing between these possibilities, as it were, making his art, like his narrator's racial identity, a fluid medium in which the culture of race could be expressed and studied.

The whole of Johnson's novel is a study of cultural preservation, not least because it rewrites the genres of slave narrative and autobiography that had been the key African-American publications in the nineteenth century, climaxing in the *Life and Times of Frederick Douglass* (1887; revised 1892), *Up From Slavery* (1901), and *The Souls of Black Folk*. But it is not simply the novel's anonymity or its recasting of the exceptional lives of Frederick Douglass, Booker T. Washington, and W. E. B. Du Bois that gives

The Autobiography of an Ex-Coloured Man its unusually complicated perspective. Those tactics, along with the brittle quality of
Johnson's language, support another noteworthy feature of the
novel—its relationship to Johnson's work as a songwriter and his
penetrating commentary on African-American music and poetry.
The unorthodox narrative premise of the novel allowed Johnson
to explore ideas that he would later expand upon in essays and
prefaces, but it did so by allowing him at the same time to distill
pragmatism from adulation, to see the black folk culture of slavery
as the origin and harbinger of modern African-American art while
arguing both the necessity and the danger of its transformation
into broader American idioms.

·   ·   ·

There is hardly a passage of Johnson's novel in which the
chameleonlike language of the narrative does not offer a good
opportunity to measure his strange combination of fiction and
cultural analysis. But perhaps the most challenging sustained episode occurs in the climactic chapter 10, where the narrator under-
takes his ritual descent into southern black culture, with the initial
intention of collecting and publishing the African-American folklore and spirituals that Johnson, among others, estimated to be
the most significant *American* culture to date. The entire chapter, issuing in the lynching scene that drives the narrator over
the color line, puts Johnson's diverse rhetorical strategies on display. As is often the case in the novel, the language throughout
this chapter changes color, so to speak, paragraph by paragraph,
even line by line, as the narrator's analysis of race, class, and
folk culture, borne along by a perspective and style of quizzical
anthropological detachment, slowly gives way to the explosively
complicated spectacle of lynching and the narrator's moral ruin.
The compact sequence of events that leads to the lynching, once

the narrator has reached Macon, Georgia, forms one of the most significant statements of cultural deformation and resistance in modern African-American literature; but two other scenes in the early part of the chapter are also worth special notice.

Here, as elsewhere, the Ex-Coloured Man's voice is a screen not only for his maneuvering but also for Johnson's gift for condensing diverse, conflicting cultural forces into moments of ritual intensity. Thus, the narrator's contention that the "more active elements of the race" marry lighter out of "natural" inclination and "economic necessity"—part of his ongoing self-serving argument about color and class relations—has a plausible ring despite its inaccuracy. Likewise, his claim that it is no more "a sacrifice of self-respect" for a black man to give his children the advantage of color than for a rich man to give his children the advantage of wealth is simultaneously credible and repulsive. This meditation on "marriage selection" of course forecasts and seeks to justify the choice the protagonist will make—or rather, has already made by the time he writes his narrative—but the manner in which Johnson punctuates this little essay is characteristic of his extraordinary skill at shifting his narrative surreptitiously into a volatile new mode: "I once heard a coloured man sum it up in these words," says the narrator: "'It's no disgrace to be black, but it's often very inconvenient.'"

The unacknowledged "coloured man" who spoke these words as part of his famous stage routine was Bert Williams, along with his partner George Walker one of the best-known and most innovative black minstrel performers of the day. In appropriating Williams's deft signifying on Jim Crow, Johnson released his protagonist and his own complex critique of segregated America into a minefield of irony. Masked as the shuffling darky figure on stage, Williams, who was rather light skinned, epitomized the painful truth of blackface minstrelsy stated by Walker: "Nothing seemed more absurd than to see a colored man making himself ridiculous in order to portray himself." As both Walker and Williams contended, however, black minstrelsy was a double-edged sword. The reappropriation of minstrelsy by African-American performers at the end of the nineteenth century accelerated their access to legitimate stage and musical careers, while extending a tradition of performative subversion of white authority that reached back into slave culture. Black dance, black storytelling, and black speech in America were nurtured in a state of frequently satiric opposition or disguised insubordination, and modern minstrelsy thus raised such dissent to a high art even as it risked perpetuating the crude, racist stereotypes of "coon" songs and neo-Confederate plantation romance. In advertising themselves as "real coons," Williams and Walker both adopted and subverted stereotypes—not least, it might be added, because their claim to authenticity had such an unusual source. When the actual Dahomean dancers who had been engaged to appear in an exhibit at the San Francisco Midwinter Fair were late, black Americans, including Williams and Walker, were hired as "sham native Dahomians," Walker recalled, to play their parts. Once the real Africans arrived, Williams and Walker stayed on to study the Dahomeans to better delineate their mannerisms. Playing roles within roles, the minstrel team of Williams and Walker was a caricature of African retentions staged as burlesque reversion to type, both traits rendered "authentic" by being reclaimed from the travesty of blackface minstrelsy perpetrated by white performers.

Williams's deadpan remark about the "inconvenience" of being black therefore immediately thrusts the Ex-Coloured Man into something of an allegorical mode, opening to view the paradoxical political and cultural structures of racism that constitute the category of "real coon." It does not seem a mere coincidence that the narrator's anonymity in the novel archly reproduces the forlorn stage character that became Williams's trademark when in 1905—virtually the moment Johnson began writing *The Autobiography of an Ex-Coloured Man*—he introduced his best-known song, "Nobody." The lyrics of the song ("I ain't never done nothin' to nobody, / I ain't never got nothin' from nobody, no time. / Until I get somethin' from somebody, some time, / I'll never do nothin' for nobody, no time.") were played by Williams for pathos and light burlesque. But Johnson's cunning invocation of Williams's performance marks the subversive undercurrent that African-American blackface often contained: in the America of Jim Crow, to be black was always to wear the distorted mask of blackness before the white world and to be, in legal and political terms, "nobody." To be black, in relation to the dominant white culture, was to be "anonymous," as Johnson has it, to be "nothing," as several of Charles Chesnutt's penetrating short stories had argued, or to be an "invisible man," as Ralph Ellison would later contend in his own borrowing from Johnson's plot. Williams's "nobody" was an act fraught with concealed political significance that turned on ironic inversion of the sort that Johnson's novel exploits. Deciding that it is both inconvenient *and* a disgrace to be black, Johnson's protagonist becomes "nobody" in passing for white, sacrificing his birthright in order to pass on to his children a dubious heritage of visible whiteness; and it is he, not Williams, who most plays the minstrel, the pathetic costumed creation of a racist society. If his choice is "natural," it is also taken at the cost of his own shame and disgrace.

The proof is not far to seek. As chapter 10 unfolds, the narrator summarily recounts his visits to Howard University, to Fisk University and a black newspaper office in Nashville, and to Atlanta University, where he had previously been a student, before resuming his journey to Macon. All these acts would indicate that the narrator presents himself as a black man. And yet on the important train ride from Nashville to Atlanta, where he witnesses a vociferous argument about the race question between a Florida Jew, a former Union soldier, an Ohio-born southern university professor, and a Texan, the narrator changes—or one should say, loses—his color without so much as a mention of it. The scene recapitulates earlier instances of the narrator's detached observance and his general cowardice in the face of racism; in particular it points forward to the climactic lynching scene in which he will be the spectator par excellence. More important here, however, is Johnson's brilliant signifying on the ironies of segregation. His protagonist does not ride Jim Crow on this train but sits passively in the privileged spectatorial role of a "white" man while eavesdropping on this staged argument, especially the Texan's gentlemanly rantings about black inferiority and the threat of miscegenation, which are quoted at length. If he is no more a coward than the Ohio-born professor, who has, like the North in general, turned handling of the "Negro problem" over to the South, Johnson's narrator is the very sign of that sectional capitulation.

The Ex-Coloured Man is, in fact, nothing less than a mock Homer Plessy, whose own challenge to train-car segregation brought forth from the United States Supreme Court the landmark 1896 ruling in favor of Jim Crow in *Plessy* v. *Ferguson*. For Homer Plessy incarnated the absurd limits to which respect of the color line might be taken in the fact that he himself was also light enough to pass for white, so light that he had to announce to the conductor that he was black so as to test the train car law. Unlike Homer Plessy, Johnson's protagonist does not publicly announce that he is black. Far from it, he admits to feeling, beneath the chill cast by the Texan's racist diatribe, "a certain sort of admiration for the man who could not be swayed from what he held as his principles." This appears to be another example of the narrator's perverse self-justification; and yet his assertion that the Texan's overt bigotry is preferable to the pitiable ambivalence of the Ohio professor is something to the point. The politics of reunion, forged through the decline of black civil rights after Reconstruction, required northern capitulation to *national*, rather than sectional, racism. Like many of the narrator's pronouncements, his admiration for the Texan's staunch principles of white supremacy lays a mask of pragmatic rationalization over an ennervating instance of moral blindness. When he goes on to compare white racism to an incorrect astronomical calculation—whites believe the universe revolves about them, as though planets could be proved to revolve about the earth—that could be solved by application of the "simple rules of justice," the narrator's argument dissolves into an abstraction ludicrously removed from the pain and passion of racism but perfectly in keeping with his convenient alienation from his race.

The narrator's train ride repeats comparable black ritual journeys into the South—Du Bois's in *The Souls of Black Folk*, for example, or William Miller's in Chesnutt's *The Marrow of Tradition* (1901), although they both pointedly ride Jim Crow—and the train itself, the vehicle of migration and a charged icon of escape, salvation, and transcendence in the tradition of black spirituals and blues, is inherently a vibrant field of African-American cultural meanings, one that Sterling Brown, Zora Neale Hurston, and others would make a key point of reference in their vernacular art. In the wake of *Plessy* v. *Ferguson*, the train was an epitome of segregation's extensive destruction of safe public space and a virtual embodiment of racial incoherence. The landmark court cases leading to, and including, *Plessy* deduced racism from the "laws of nature," and one of *Plessy*'s own litigants, the civil rights crusader Albion Tourgée, was compelled to argue that Homer Plessy's exclusion from the Louisiana train car deprived him of his "property"—namely, his white-colored skin. The choice of material comfort and genealogical advantage made by the protagonist at the conclusion of *The Autobiography of an Ex-Coloured Man* indicates how astute Tourgée had been. Conceived as a racial mission to preserve the culture of his people, the protagonist's descent into the South—an "aborted immersion ritual," as Robert Stepto calls it—has failed even before it begins.

Already deeply written into the national contest over racial segregation, a palpable sign of betrayal for black and white alike, Johnson's narrator arrives in Macon, where, like a European explorer in colonial Africa, he deposits his trunk and belongings and, as he puts it, "strike[s] out into the interior." The analogy of imperial exploration is apt, for this simple phrase, like so many others in the novel, maps onto the narrative action a constellation of cultural implications that locate Johnson's protagonist at a historical moment of great racial upheaval, asking us to see the potential disappearance of African-American culture under the pressures of harsh segregation and race violence in terms at least vaguely synonymous with the colonial decimation of African culture. His travel to rural Georgia is, in fact, an imperial incursion of sorts. Based loosely on Johnson's summer of rural teaching while he was a student at Atlanta University, the journey to the interior reflects on that experience in a profound way while also rewriting the similar example of Du Bois's own sojourn in rural Georgia, which had provided the framework for some of his most powerful writing in *The Souls of Black Folk*. Du Bois also wrote as a middle-class outsider (and a northerner to boot), but by an act of will and brilliant analysis he was able to make himself, as he wrote, "bone of the bone and flesh of the flesh of them that live within the Veil." Johnson's narrator is able to do nothing of the sort. His overtly ethnological perspective derives from his own self-protecting disengagement from rural black culture—both its physical and economic dangers, but more importantly, from Johnson's point of view, its cultural demands. Indeed, the burden of chapter 10 is to demonstrate simultaneously the distance that Johnson has on his cowardly protagonist *and* the degree to which he stands in judgment on those characteristics that he has in common with him.

The Ex-Coloured Man's brief compliment to Du Bois for his efforts to break down cultural traditions of bigotry ("A beginning has already been made in that remarkable book by Dr. Du Bois, *The Souls of Black Folk*") appears to register both the narrator's occluded vision of Du Bois's towering achievement and the authorial anxiety attendant upon Johnson's own admiration of Du Bois's book (in *Along This Way* Johnson reiterated his opinion that *The Souls of Black Folk*, with its "brooding but intransigent spirit," had a greater impact on black Americans than any book since *Uncle Tom's Cabin*). Johnson could not surpass Du Bois's scintillating analysis of Black Belt culture passed through the furnace of post-Reconstruction violence and the new slavery of sharecropping, nor could he compose a text that made his work so much of a piece with slave culture and the world of African survivals as had Du Bois in his use of the spirituals. Instead, he used the extreme moral ambivalence of his narrator to engage the power, historical importance, and beauty of vernacular culture while at the same time carefully estimating its certain erosion in the face of recurrent racism, generational change, and the pressure of commercial assimilation. In doing so, Johnson took the measure of his own career first as a lyricist and later as an advocate of African-American music, in both of which roles he sought to cross the color line, transfiguring the voices of slave culture into the sounds of modern American art. He looked backward and forward in his career, one might say, and the climactic scenes of chapter 10, which initiate the narrator's final decision to pass, superimpose at least three levels of action: the narrator's moral crisis, the ethnographic debate over the legitimacy of African-American culture, and Johnson's own anxiety about his generation's declension from the power and "authenticity" of vernacular slave culture.

．　．　．

Along with his brother Rosamond as composer and their other partner, Bob Cole, Johnson belonged to the generation of musicians whose work for the black stage significantly transcended the crudest coon song stereotypes of the day. Although the compositions of the Johnson brothers and Cole were intended for, and appealed to, a comparatively broad, non-racialized audience, the national color line could not be entirely erased, nor could songwriters avoid sacrificing the best traits of vernacular art along with its worst. Bob Cole explained that the songwriting team aimed to "evolve a type of music that will have all that is distinct in the old Negro music and yet which will be sophisticated enough to appeal to the cultured musician. We want the Negro spirit—its warmth and originality—to color our music; we want to retain its marked rhythms, but we are trying to get away from that minor strain that used to dominate it." Before James Weldon Johnson left his partners in 1906 to accept a consular appointment to Venezuela, the trio had reaped significant profits from such tunes as "My Castle on the Nile," "Congo Love Song," and their best-known composition, "Under the Bamboo Tree," which incorporated the modified harmonic structure and rhythm of "Nobody Knows the Trouble I've Seen." The echoes of minstrelsy that appeared in early black musicals and, notably here, the incorporation of elements from the tradition of African-American spirituals into American popular music were part of a larger pattern of collection, transmutation, and assimilation that marked the evolution of African-American culture, particularly folklore and music, in the aftermath of slavery.

The tension that Cole noted between the "old Negro music" and work that might "appeal to the cultured musician" was just the tension that arrangers and publishers of black spirituals had noted with increasing urgency by the turn of the century and which Johnson built into his novel in a powerful fashion. Both the climactic episodes of *The Autobiography of an Ex-Coloured Man* and Johnson's own exceptional commentary on African-American vernacular music in his two collections of black spirituals, as well as his attempt to extend its sound and cadence into a semi-vernacular verse in *God's Trombones* (1927), exhibit that conflict of cultural intentions at its height. In the novel, the unsatisfactory resolution of the conflict is figured in the protagonist's marriage and assimilation into the pallid, deadening world of white wealth and white culture. The prototype of both the promise and the failure of his negotiation between oppositional racial worlds appears in the protagonist's fragmentary childhood memories and again in his subsequent brilliant, brief career in ragtime, which functions as a strong metaphor for the cultural implications of the narrator's "dual personality" and his ultimate absorption by (and of) white culture.

According to one plausible explanation, the term ragtime derives from the idea of "ragged time," that is, a musical meter that is ragged, torn apart into conflicting rhythms by syncopation. As he proved in his landmark discussion of "swing" in the black spirituals, which he found to be related to but distinguishable from the rhythm of black work songs, Johnson himself readily told the difference between true metrical innovation and the sometimes labored intricacies of ragtime. Even so, the notion of "ragged time" serves particularly well to characterize the dilemma of the narrator. If the hallmark of ragtime is the imposition of an irregular melodic right hand upon a more regular left—most frequently a variable rhythmic pattern of three against two that, in Gunther

Schuller's words, shows the black musician "asserting an irrepressible urge to maintain two rhythms simultaneously *within* the white man's musical framework"—one might contend that the Ex-Coloured Man has chosen an art emblematic of his racial hybridity. At the same time, however, his musical talent is accompanied by no evident awareness of the black origins of the music he plays; and he himself is marked by pronounced historical disjunctions, an obliviousness to the racial past in which his double identity, rather than producing fruitful symbiosis, results at last in a deliberate cultural amnesia.

Even though the greatest crisis of conscience that this deployment of "ragged" historical time creates will not appear until the narrator's ritual immersion in the Black Belt, its origins are apparent in his first recollections about music. Whether it be taken as a symptom of the narrator's dullness, an index of his retrospective need to mask his identity, or a sign of the weakening heritage of slave culture, the portrait of his mother's playing of the spirituals is deliberately muted. Identified simply as "some old Southern songs" that she will occasionally play from memory, by ear, in place of her usual published hymns, the invisibility of the spirituals is a function not only of the mother's own interracial dilemma as the daughter of miscegenation and the forsaken lover of a white man, but also of the generational erosion of the songs' immediacy. Embued with sentiment and maternal protectiveness, the narrator's memory of his mother "crooning some old melody without words" recomposes a central scene in *The Souls of Black Folk* with saccharine irony. In a scene of resonant inventiveness, Du Bois had recalled his great-great-grandmother singing "Do bana coba," a purportedly African song whose untranslatable words—which Du Bois believed to be a Bantu language but which in fact are nonsensical—thrust his search for the origins of African-American culture into a mythic African past. Her African song has travelled down the generations for two hundred years, Du Bois writes, "and we sing it to our children, knowing as little as our fathers what its words may mean, but knowing well the meaning of its music."

In Du Bois's case, the wordless music supports his argument that the music of African America in the spirituals "is far more ancient than the words." Moreover, the words' very lack of meaning alludes to the loss of ancestral language—or, perhaps, to its slight, fragmentary survival in the words and phrases that have entered American English. Whereas the African words of "Do bana coba" represent a signifying reminder that English was a borrowed language, the basis for marvelous cultural invention but still an alien tongue for the generations of African Americans brought to the Americas in the course of the slave trade, the "melody without words" sung by the protagonist's mother in *The Autobiography of an Ex-Coloured Man* marks not even the equivocal access to a racial past but rather an alienation from it. "I can see her now," says the narrator, "her great dark eyes looking into the fire, to where? No one knew but her." The truncated scene disappears into a past with no articulated dimensions; it intimates longing and memory but does not record them, instead participating in the narrator's obliteration of his racial history. The "place of purity and safety in which her arms held me," all that remains to the narrator, is notable precisely because it does *not,* as in the case of Du Bois, take on the strong connotation of maternal racial inheritance, the ancestral principle of mother Africa laid upon the severities and genealogical imperatives of plantation slavery, and doubly encoded into spirituals such as "Sometimes I Feel Like a Motherless Child." On the contrary, the narrator recovers the semblance of this maternal affection, for what it is worth, not by succeeding in his preservation of slave culture but by blotting it out in his marriage to a white woman.

Well before he decides to pass, then—in fact, even before he leaves home—the narrator has been effectively stripped of his mother's ancestral culture. The striking passage that deliberately confuses his mother with the teacher who first reminds him publicly of the fact that he is "colored" ("I have never forgiven the woman who did it so cruelly") is laden with ghostly recriminations ostensibly directed against his mother and father but ultimately referring to the potential extinguishing of black culture. Like Roxy in Twain's *Pudd'nhead Wilson* (1894), another precursor text recapitulated by Johnson, the narrator's equally white-skinned mother has absorbed the logic of Jim Crow. "Your father is one of the greatest men in the country—the best blood of the South is in you," she haltingly tells her son. His anonymous white father, defined metonymically by his gold watch and chain, his polished shoes, and his hewing to the color line of "custom and law" codified in *Plessy*, does not claim the boy as his son or, once the mother has died, follow through on his promise to send him to Harvard. The gold coin he hangs around his son's neck is the chain of neoslavery—rendered worthless by the hole drilled through it but nonetheless symbolic of the property of whiteness, the "mess of pottage," that the narrator will eventually claim as his inheritance.

What Johnson adds to this near caricature of miscegenation's family romance, borrowed from the fiction of the tragic mulatto and from slave narratives, notably those of Frederick Douglass, is the clarity of cultural allegory. "I found it impossible to frame the word 'father,'" writes the Ex-Coloured Man, echoing Douglass's assertion about his white father in *My Bondage and My Freedom*: "I say nothing of *father*, for he is shrouded in a mystery I have never been able to penetrate. Slavery does away with fathers, as it does away with families." In Johnson's reiteration of slavery's fracturing of the African family, here under the new slavery of segregation, the narrator can find neither white fathers nor black, and he reproduces his "white" mother in a white wife who gives him "white" children then conveniently dies, taking his racial secret to her grave. The past that the narrator strains to recover but ultimately renounces is itself placed beneath the color line: if black culture became white enough, it might pass, but the one-drop rule always threatened to prove that the law of Jim Crow was everywhere prohibitive, liberating only in a way that was equally illusive and immoral. In the long run, by the time he had written *God's Trombones* and collected the two books of spirituals, Johnson had made a signal contribution to preserving the essential elements of slave culture. When he wrote his novel, however, he may have been secretly anxious about the decay of African-American expressive forms at the hands of those, like himself, who had transfigured them into commercial success in the white world. It is not irrelevant, of course, that the white patron who guarantees the protagonist's success as a ragtime pianist is parodied as both a subsequent father figure and a cultural slaveholder: "He seemed to be some grim, mute, but relentless tyrant, possessing over me a supernatural power which he used to drive me on mercilessly to exhaustion." Both the patron's good pay and the narrator's fawning, semifilial admiration for the man's power preclude the flowering of the racial resentment that lies barely concealed in Johnson's evasive prose but which the narrator must strictly repress from his own consciousness.

It is appropriate, then, that the Ex-Coloured Man be specifically adept at ragtime, a liminal art whose paradoxes made it at once innovative and stultifying. The episodes of the novel devoted to ragtime throw a sharp light both on the protagonist's failure to assist in the preservation of southern black music and on Johnson's doubts about the very possibility of doing so. Johnson was not alone in recognizing that ragtime originated with black piano players of the South and Midwest, artists (as he wrote in a statement that deserves careful examination) who played by "natural musical instinct" and "extraordinary sense of rhythm," but "did not know any more about the theory of music than they did about the theory of the universe." The modulation of folk art into genius, a process in which one might deduce a vernacular rather than a formal "theory of music," in this case reveals both the advent and debasement of one genre of black American music. Although it is possible to trace the syncopation of ragtime to an imposition of African polyrhythms upon the more regular meter and rhythm of European musical forms, and to locate its originating elements in black dance and work songs as they evolved through the cakewalk, commercial ragtime easily lost its fundamental African-American character. It had an important role in the evolution of instrumental jazz, but in its most widely exploited forms—when it became "national rather than racial," as Johnson put it—ragtime was often a composed, mechanical music. As in the case of other popular musical idioms, black ragtime composers frequently saw their work appropriated, or stolen outright, by white artists and publishers. No sooner had ragtime allowed African-American musicians a pathway of escape from the racism of minstrelsy than it fell into banal popularization by northern white entrepreneurs, a historical trajectory that is essentially recapitulated in the musical life of the Ex-Coloured Man.

From the beginning of his career as a pianist, the protagonist appears to us as a figure adept at improvisation. In his youth he evinces a "particular fondness for the black keys," and he inserts "strange harmonies" into his mother's rendition of black spirituals. His teacher has "no small difficulty at first in pinning [him] down to the notes," and he goes on to associate his capacity for improvisation with an equal talent for rewriting the plots of stories—such as his own "autobiography," we are to understand.

The protagonist's inclination toward blue tonality and improvisation may be taken as a sign of his tricksterism, his existence in the liminal territory between authorized cultural forms and languages. However, rather than marking him as an original, like the New York ragtime player who later proves to be his inspiration, the Ex-Coloured Man's talent—more so, perhaps, his literary talent—instead resembles that of "the modern innovators who strive after originality by seeing how cleverly they can dodge about through the rules of harmony and at the same time avoid melody." If this is Johnson's potshot at early jazz, which was providing a way out of ragtime's blind alley, it is also a good analogy for the protagonist's devious narrative, though not for his musical talents, which are in the end sacrificed to conformity and race betrayal. Occupying a musical space divided by a hypothetical color line—and divided by estimates of artistic achievement that continue today to provoke serious musicological debate—ragtime is perfectly suited to the character and iconographic meaning of Johnson's protagonist, whose blackness dissolves in disgrace and whose intention to promote the vernacular culture of African Americans is ultimately reduced to a box of unpublished "yellowing manuscripts."

Black American music, as Johnson well knew, could not easily escape Jim Crow. Even as it became assimilated to simplified formulas, ragtime did not lose its reputation among many commentators of being "barbarous," "savage," or "primitive"—that is, of being essentially "black," with all the danger such cultural miscegenation might imply. Like the cakewalk and coon songs from which it partly derived, ragtime was both innovative and imitative: it was often technically *parodic,* freighted with notions of subversion and contamination. The creation of original ragtime tunes was deemed bad enough, but the far greater threat lay in the fact, as much appreciated by the public as it was deprecated by prim observers, that ragtime was a technique applicable to virtually all music. Both the democratic popularity and the technical cul-de-sac of ragtime lay in the fact that any song could be "ragged," and Eubie Blake and others owed a good deal of their popularity to the ragging of standards. "It is no uncommon thing in these days of rampant frivolity and seemingly almost universal imbecility," wrote Edward Baxter Perry in the staid *Etude* magazine in 1918, to hear "good compositions by recognized composers of high standing perverted and distorted out of all semblance to the original works and vulgarized beyond the power of language to express by being changed and twisted into cheap ragtime rhythms." A sign of complete cultural decadence, Perry contended, ragtime "is syncopation gone mad, and its victims . . . can only be treated successfully like the dog with rabies, with a dose of lead." Such a reaction, comic in its exaggeration, need not be seen to foreground race. Yet there is no doubt that race is implicit in Perry's metaphors of madness and infection, which would be repeated in subsequent lurid attacks on jazz, on rock 'n' roll, and more recently on rap music. A music in which "the wires of dark and white America crossed and the vital currents were flowing back and forth," as Rudi Blesh has written, ragtime was a music of amalgamation, and it therefore occupies a highly charged domain of double identity appropriate to the amorphous narrator, who becomes the best ragtime pianist in turn-of-the-century New York—not by composing original tunes but by being the first to rag classics, such as Mendelssohn's "Wedding March," which he says never failed to arouse enthusiastic response at the club where he plays and which also points ahead, of course, to his literal marriage and physiological incorporation into white culture.

As it happens, Johnson and many of his readers would have known that a popular rag version of the "Wedding March" had been published in 1902 by Axel Christensen, the best-known writer of the ragtime instruction books that proliferated around the turn of the century, beginning with Ben Harney's *Rag Time Instructor* in 1897. Multiple editions of Christensen's instruction books and storefront schools devoted to his simple method made him the leading popularizer of ragtime, in the process dwarfing the efforts of serious composers like Scott Joplin to demonstrate the difference between classic ragtime, with its firm roots in the black South, and the typically degraded work promoted by mercenaries like Christensen. When he implicitly identifies his protagonist's talent with the school of Christensen rather than Joplin—makes it referentially northern and white rather than southern and black, as it were—Johnson opens the possibility that we are to read this as straightforward irony, the narrator's talent in keeping with his moral cowardice. Although commentators have attempted to distinguish black and white ragtime on the basis of metrical and rhythmic features, such efforts usually seem hazy and tendentious. Johnson himself was loath to draw a stylistic color line, even though he was clear about the origins of the best American music and the fact that cultural miscegenation had already occurred in the most profound way by the passing of black music—spirituals, ragtime, and the blues—into white American music. He would later write in *Along This Way* (1933) that "in his lighter music . . . the Negro has given America its best-known distinctive form of art," a statement that referred primarily to the musical stage and cabaret jazz but which excluded neither the ragging of white standards nor, more importantly, the kind of appropriation that he and Rosamond engaged in when they took the melody of an anonymous black southern folk song—one of those "jes' grew" songs he describes in the *Book of American Negro Poetry*—and turned it into "Oh, Didn't He Ramble!"

In Johnson's novel, such cultural negotiations are at once foregrounded and made opaque, and the true fascination lies in the fact that it is so hard to tell exactly how to interpret either the narrator's talent or his opinions about music. When read in the context of the preface to the *Book of American Negro Poetry*, to take a prominent example, Johnson's remark about black ragtime pianists knowing no more about the theory of music than the theory of the universe sounds less pejorative than it does in the mouth of the novel's smug narrator. Still, it betrays in Johnson himself a residual aesthetic distrust of the folk, a belief in the need to press vernacular art into the mold of European forms in order to raise it to a higher level. What one notes most of all about Johnson's well-known argument that the cakewalk, ragtime, Uncle Remus tales, and Jubilee songs are essential American art forms—a view put forth first in *The Autobiography of an Ex-Coloured Man* before being elaborated in his preface to the *Book of American Negro Poetry*—is that Johnson's admiration unites populism and elitism. "These are lower forms of art," he writes in the novel, "but they give evidence of a power that will some day be applied to the higher forms." Virtually the same sentence again occurs in the later preface, as do other remarks about ragtime and the spirituals, which turn up once more in the prefaces to the two collections of spirituals. There is no doubt that Johnson's theory was in large part a reaction to the vulgarization of black music, not to mention the denial of black social and political aspirations, in minstrelsy and plantation romance. But it was a serious question whether one could, as Bob Cole advocated, have a new music that actually preserved the "old Negro music" while at the same time appealing to more "sophisticated" tastes. The great tension between inherited slave culture and the "higher forms" of artistic work is embodied in Johnson's problematic aesthetic, which because of its articulation in several different formats offers a kind of archeological record of the process of assimilation through which cultures both evolve and disappear.

It would be far too strong to say that his advocacy of the spirituals was a kind of penance for his career in popular music, but it was in that work that Johnson most allied himself with the ancestral roots of modern African-American culture, the fathers that the Ex-Coloured Man can never locate and the culture that he betrays. As I suggest in chapter 2 of this book, one can witness in Zora Neale Hurston's transfiguration of the Lovelace sermon, taken from her folkloric prose, into John Pearson's sermon a virtuoso performance of fictive creation. In the case of Johnson, however, one is presented with nearly the reverse problem: the novel precedes the prose statements, and the challenge is to identify and estimate the curious mixture of sincerity, parodic undercurrent, and unconscious revelation manifest in the narrator's voicing of opinions so much like Johnson's own, but in a novelistic context so loaded with ironies and contradictions. That the novel precedes the prose statements therefore also adds a further dimension of "ragged time" that requires special attention.

．　．　．

The passage from *Along This Way* in which Johnson compliments Negro popular music concludes with his humorous observation that the spectacle of white people dancing to black music in Harlem, "attempting to throw off the crusts and layers of inhibitions laid on by sophisticated civilization," is a sign of their need "to work their way back into that jungle which was the original Garden of Eden; in a word, doing their best to pass for colored." The archetypal nod to primitivism is of less note here than the allusion to passing, which might also appear incidental were it not for *The Autobiography of an Ex-Coloured Man* (which had been reissued with Johnson's name attached in 1927) and for the counterstatement Hurston was to make some years later in her acerbic autobiography, *Dust Tracks on the Road*:

This passing business works both ways. All the passing is not passing for white. We have white folks among us passing for colored. They just happened to be born with a tinge of brown in the skin and took up being colored as a profession. Take James Weldon Johnson, for instance.

There's a man white enough to suit Hitler, and he's been passing for colored for years.

Now, don't get the idea that he is not welcome among us. He certainly is. He has more than paid his way. But he just is not a negro. . . .

Hurston's biting comment, not uncharacteristic of the heterodox opinions of her autobiography, must be taken with a grain of salt. She was friendly with Johnson in the 1920s and 1930s, and, comparing it to her own experiment with the Lovelace sermon, she wrote favorably of his attempt to meld folk poetry and conventional written verse in *God's Trombones*. Quite possibly it was Johnson's cultivated, urbane manner, his easy travel in privileged circles, or even his comparatively light color and somewhat Hispanic features that sparked her comic remark. Certainly it was not any lack of devotion to the cause of black civil rights, social equality, and African-American culture on his part. Most likely, it was the decided aesthetic gulf between Johnson and Hurston that better explains her satiric barb.

Over the course of turn-of-the-century debates about the ethnological and artistic value of the spirituals, the most frequently argued issue was the "authenticity" of the songs, both the music itself and to a lesser degree the words, a debate which in turn veered off into discussions of the propriety of reproducing black dialect in verse, folklore, and fiction. Hurston for her part took an extreme view that had valuable consequences for her writing but was also idealistic to the point of being mannered. "There never has been a presentation of genuine Negro spirituals to any audience anywhere," she wrote in her essay "Spirituals and Neo-

Spirituals," which appeared in Nancy Cunard's collection *Negro: An Anthology* in 1934. She included the Johnson brothers in a list of distinguished arrangers and performers of neospirituals—that is, concertized or published versions based on the originals—whose work she applauded but carefully distinguished in musical terms from the dissonances, wavers, chants, and irregularities of black folk singing: "Let no one imagine that [the neospirituals] are the songs of the people, as sung by them." Hurston's essay also includes commentary on the straining voice of the black preacher that is indispensable for distinguishing her rendition of folk verse from Johnson's, but her purist's view of the spirituals caps an already lengthy tradition of comments dating to antebellum collectors that is worth brief summary.

Beginning with such early collectors as William Allen and Lucy and James Miller McKim, the ethnography on slave spirituals frequently regretted the difficulty of recording and preserving them accurately. As Allen remarked in his preface to the landmark 1867 collection *Slave Songs in the United States*, "The best that we can do . . . with paper and types, or even with voices, will convey but a faint shadow of the original. The voices of the colored people have a peculiar quality that nothing can imitate; and the intonations and delicate variations of even one singer cannot be reproduced on paper. And I despair of conveying any notion of the effect of a number singing together, especially in a complicated shout." In one sense little had changed by 1903 (the year *The Souls of Black Folk* was published) when Charles Peabody, writing in the *Journal of American Folklore*, included the example of a black Mississippi man's work song periodically "intoned" as he plowed behind a mule for fifteen hours a day, producing a song that "melted into strains of apparently genuine African music, sometimes with words, sometimes without. Long phrases there were without apparent measured rhythms, singularly hard to copy in notes." Similarly, Peabody discovered that a black woman's lullaby was "quite impossible to copy, weird in interval and strange in rhythm; peculiarly beautiful." Even if theorists became more adept at hearing and transcribing black song, however, the assimilating process of transcription and concertization took its toll. As Du Bois argued in *The Souls of Black Folk*, numerous performing groups, seeking to emulate the famous Fisk Jubilee Singers, had "filled the air with debased melodies which vulgar ears scarce know from the real." Well before the end of the century the difficulty of properly annotating the "real" spirituals was thus compounded by the obverse difficulty introduced by concert and published versions that simplified the songs, forcing them into a regularized tempo and the more rigid mold of the European tempered scale. According to Thomas Fenner, musical director at Hampton Institute and arranger of one of the two well-known collections of spirituals on which Du Bois evidently relied in his choice and analysis of the sorrow songs in *The Souls of Black Folk*, as did Johnson a generation later, so little of the spirit that created black music could be "transported to the boards of a public performance" that it became a difficult question whether or not one could transcribe and arrange the music for choral presentation "without destroying its original characteristics."

Collectors and arrangers who sought to preserve "this wonderful music of bondage," as Fenner put it in an appropriately paradoxical phrase, were thus caught in a double bind. Even though spirituals were being gathered and published in great quantities by the turn of the century, this activity was accompanied by an overwhelming sense that black music was about to disappear as the older generations died and as the middle class sought to distance itself from all reminders of slavery, preferring, as Johnson's protagonist puts it, to sing "hymns from books." Transcriptions and popularized arrangements inevitably diluted, even eviscerated the original sounds of the spirituals—the slides, wavers, shouts, blue tonality, and swing, the "harmony and disharmony, the shifting keys and broken time" that Hurston found to be characteristic. Nathaniel Dett concluded the preface to his own influential collection of "neo-spirituals" (he too was on Hurston's list) with the observation that contemporary versions and their singers suffered not just because of their distance from antebellum slavery but more particularly from "the influence of the white man's education, of the concert-hall, the phonograph, and the radio." He thought that the best that could be hoped for was a slight recovery of "the depth, sincerety, and pathos which marked [the singing] of the other days." More emphatically, an elderly Kentucky woman interviewed by Jeanette Robinson Murphy delivered a vivid jeremiad against the declension of black faith and black music in the younger generations: "Dese spirituals am de best moanin' music in de world, case dey is de whole Bible sung out and out. Notes is good enough for you people, but us likes a mixtery. Dese young heads ain't wuth killin', fur dey don't keer bout de Bible nor de ole hymns. Dey's completely spiled wid too much white blood in 'em, and de big organ and de eddication has done took all de Holy Spirit out en 'em, till dey ain't no better wid der dances and cuttin' up dan de white folks." This account would no doubt have pleased Hurston. For his part, Johnson might have appreciated the spirit of such a view, but he would also have taken it as a relic of thought best honored by the elevation of "moanin' music" into what he took to be more cultivated forms.

The argument between Johnson and Hurston over the nature of the spirituals may be one as much of nuance as of substance— and yet nuance is all. In his rich commentary on the spirituals in the two books of American Negro spirituals, and even in the unstable voice of his protagonist in *The Autobiography of an Ex-Coloured Man*, Johnson offered perhaps the most commanding account of them to date. Although he did not embroil himself very deeply in the contentious issue of African survivals in the spirituals, except to trace some elements of rhythm, dialect, and call-and-response form to African influences, Johnson dismissed as absurd the widespread contemporary argument that the spirituals were borrowed wholesale from white Protestant models: "The white people among whom the slaves lived did not originate anything comparable even to the mere titles of the Spirituals." At the same time, Johnson disputed the notion put forward by black commentators like Hurston and Kelly Miller, or white commentators like Carl Van Vechten, that whites could not possibly sing spirituals or play black music properly. Europeans, because they mistakenly "play the notes too correctly, and do not play what is not written down," typically produce ludicrous results, Johnson noted, but white Americans, he thought, might do better. The key in any case is to know and feel the truth of the origins of black songs, "to realize something of what they have meant in the experiences of the people who created them."

It is here, however, that the fundamental if finely graduated difference between Johnson and Hurston would arise. And it is a difference that is noticeable in their very styles of speaking of virtually the same phenomena. In his extremely perceptive discussion of "swing," for instance, Johnson nevertheless tends toward a somewhat calculated analysis: "It is subtle and elusive because it is in perfect union with the religious ecstasy that manifests itself in the swaying of the bodies of a whole congregation, swaying as if responding to the baton of some extremely sensitive conductor." And his suggestion that blacks harmonize "instinctively"— "it may be said that all male Negro youth of the United States is divided into quartets," he flippantly remarks—is directed in part toward proving that among trained black voices stridency gives way to a special "orchestral timbre." Hurston's theory of true

"*Negro* song," in contrast to the work of such performing "glee clubs," is markedly different:

> To begin with, Negro spirituals are not solo or quartette material. The jagged harmony is what makes it, and it ceases to be what it was when this is absent. Neither can any group be trained to reproduce it. Its truth dies under training like flowers under hot water. The harmony of the true spiritual is not regular. The dissonances are important and not to be ironed out by the trained musician. The various parts break in at any old time. Falsetto often takes the place of regular voices for short periods. Keys change. Moreover, each singing of the piece is a new creation. The congregation is bound by no rules. No two times singing is [*sic*] alike, so that we must consider the rendition of a song not as a final thing, but as a mood. It won't be the same thing next Sunday.

The extended accounts of Johnson and Hurston are not entirely at variance, and highlighted here are the differences rather than the similarities. The essential divergence is perhaps best summed up in their contrasting views of concertized spirituals. Whereas Johnson praised both Roland Hayes and Paul Robeson for their distinct but equally brilliant transfigurations of the spirituals into high concert art, Hurston, speaking in Chicago, took a predictably oppositional stance: "Robeson sings Negro songs better than most, because, thank God, he lacks musical education. But we have a cathead man in Florida who can sing so that if you heard him you wouldn't want to hear Hayes or Robeson. He hasn't the voice of either one. It's the effect."

The proof of both the superior power and the precariousness of Hurston's aesthetic lies in her use of the Lovelace sermon, first in Cunard's *Negro* and then in *Jonah's Gourd Vine*—although in truth, of course, the credit belongs as much to C. C. Lovelace for his language and performance as to Hurston for her arrangement of the sermon in verse. The next chapter offers a more detailed comparison between Johnson's composed sermonic verse, *God's Trombones*, and Hurston's Lovelace sermon. But the etiology of Johnson's volume bears notice for the relationship it has to *The Autobiography of an Ex-Coloured Man*. His inspiration for the first of his sermonic poems, "The Creation," came during a 1918 lecture tour on behalf of the NAACP. In Kansas City he had occasion to hear a famed black evangelist who began to preach a dull, text-bound formal sermon, perhaps out of misplaced respect for Johnson's presence. Upon sensing his audience's apathy, however, the preacher, as Johnson later recalled, suddenly "slammed the Bible shut, stepped out from behind the pulpit, and began intoning the rambling Negro sermon that begins with the creation of the world, touches various high spots in the trials and tribulations of the Hebrew children, and ends with the Judgment Day." That is to say, he preached a sermon in line with the performance of Lovelace, playing his voice as a great instrument of arousal and moving his audience to ecstatic response. The result, for Johnson, was his scribbling the first notes toward "The Creation," which was finally published in 1920. Inspiration for the remaining poems in *God's Trombones* came, he stated, in the process of collecting the spirituals and materials for his introduction to the first *Book of American Negro Spirituals*, which once again put him "in touch with the deepest revelation of the Negro's soul that has yet been made."

In both the sermonic verse of *God's Trombones* and the spirituals that he and Rosamund published—their two collections were among the best of the hundred or more published in the first decades of the century—Johnson underscored his repeated contention that American composers and authors had at hand in black vernacular song a "vast" and "unexplored mine" of rich materials. Occupying the moderate position, Johnson strenuously advocated an appreciation and preservation of the spirituals, "a gaze inward upon [their] own cultural resources" that would allow African Americans at once to put aside postemancipation skepticism and embarrassment about slave culture and to develop vernacular materials into more sophisticated art for the stage and concert hall. (Johnson's "Creation" was scored for chamber orchestra by Louis Gruenberg in 1926 under the title *The Creation: A Negro Sermon for Voice and Eight Instruments*.) In drawing such a version of the color line—if a line could be drawn at all—the question was not at what point the spirituals or their derivatives became white, but at what point they ceased to be black. From Hurston's point of view, such a "development" involved greater costs to authenticity and original racial integrity than Johnson was ready to recognize. But Hurston's friendly quarrel with Johnson appears to have been based largely on her reaction to the theoretical prefaces for his anthologies. In fact, Johnson himself had already made an equally painful and searching estimate of the costs of black cultural preservation in *The Autobiography of an Ex-Coloured Man* nearly two decades earlier.

. . .

Upon setting out among the rural folk after his arrival in Macon, the Ex-Coloured Man offers characteristically two-edged remarks about popular images of the black South. On the one hand, he attacks the "literary concept of the American Negro," the stereotyped pictures of plantation romance and minstrelsy that inhibit any true understanding among whites of African Americans. At the same time, however, he asserts that such stereotypes are an "obstacle in the way of the thoughtful and progressive element of the race," as though "coon" humor were a feature of the black lower classes themselves rather than of white racism; and he judges, paradoxically, that there is a great deal about the rural black South that does not require description since "log-cabins and plantations and dialect-speaking 'darkies' are perhaps better known in American literature than any other single picture of our national life." Here as elsewhere, the bizarre tenor of the narrator's prose, its sudden shifts of perspective, its half-ironies and abrupt revelations of class- and color-bound prejudice, cannot be adequately registered by paraphrase and brief quotation. Rather, one must allow it to unfold serially, while continually comparing the narrator's voicings to those of Johnson himself in his later theoretical works. In the *Book of American Negro Poetry*, for instance, Johnson's similar reflections on the plantation stereotypes of "log-cabin" Negroes lead into a broader argument about the problem of working in dialect. As he does once again in the later preface to *God's Trombones*, Johnson argues for the creation of a black linguistic "form that will express the racial spirit by symbols from within rather than by symbols from without," a nationalistic form that will do for African Americans what Synge did for the Irish. *God's Trombones* is a less than perfect realization of the goal, but it at least envisions a way out of the linguistic deformities of minstrelsy that haunted many turn-of-the-century black poets.

In *The Autobiography of an Ex-Coloured Man*, however, the narrator's opinions constantly veer off into self-aggrandizement or ironic denouement. Plantation romance is not transcended but internalized in the Ex-Coloured Man's racialism. Although the narrator asserts that he is no admirer of Uncle Tom, he believes that there "were lots of old Negroes as foolishly good as he." The issue, however, is not so much whether the narrator is correct—Chesnutt once remarked that he knew such faithful retainers existed among the older generation but preferred not to write about them—but what use he makes of his belief. As it turns out, of course, the narrator's remarks about Uncle Tom appear to be just as full of dissimulation as his later praise of Booker T. Washington. The narrator has none of Uncle Tom's moral strength, and his cowardice is all the more marked by his assertion that *Uncle Tom's Cabin* is a "fair and truthful panorama of slavery" that "opened my eyes as to who and what I was" and "gave me my bearing." Indeed, it is the romantic stereotypes rather than the spiritual realism of Stowe's novel that shape the narrator's self-presentation; and despite the great importance of *Uncle Tom's Cabin* among nineteenth-century black readers (one of whom Johnson must have been), it is notable that he highlights this book while granting black authors and texts by comparison only cursory notice. Likewise, the Ex-Coloured Man's just recognition of the intimacy that exists between some southern whites and blacks, in contrast to the failed ideals of northern liberalism, immediately gives way to hyperbole: "This affectionate relation between the Southern whites and those blacks who come into close touch with them has not been overdrawn even in fiction." Plantation romance and the racism on which it was frequently built offends the Ex-Coloured Man's sensibilities—but not very much. He sees instead only the artificial affections spawned in the mythology of benevolent paternalism.

The disingenuous critique of plantation romance places a kind of frame around the narrator's account of his residence in Georgia, for he recurs to it in describing his recoil from the lynching. But it also gives shape to the entire episode narrated in chapter 10, where his perspective is decidedly literary and ethnographic. The narrator's inspiration to go south comes from hearing a European pianist render ragtime in a series of classical forms. Self-interest and service to the race are combined in his plan to "go back into the very heart of the South, to live among the people, and drink in [his] inspiration firsthand" so as to create an "American music . . . based on Negro themes." Johnson later remarked in

Along This Way that it was *"in the South* that the race problem must be solved," not because the North was free from racism—far from it—but because the political status of the Negro in the South would always be the measure for the nation as a whole. He might have said the same about the recovery of African-American vernacular culture—that it would have to take place in the South, on the soil of slavery and the most deeply ingrained segregation, in order to be a true measure of black cultural resilience. Johnson's career proved that resilience, but his novel estimated its forbidding risks for the northern artist and perhaps the race as a whole. The protagonist's white patron rightly asks him: "What kind of a Negro would you make now, especially in the South?" No kind of Negro at all, as it turns out. However, the noteworthy dissonance of this passage appears not in the patron's sanctimonious, if correct, oration on the vagaries of the color line and the narrator's impermeable "white" character, but rather in the protagonist's very attitude toward black music. It is here that Johnson takes an uncomfortably penetrating look at the evolution of African-American culture that his own aesthetic requires. The development of a music "based on Negro themes"—exactly what Antonin Dvorak had proposed in his famous 1895 dictum that "the future music of America must be founded on what is called 'Negro melodies' "—presumes a stance of excavation and exploitation, which in turn skews the narrator's immersion in Black Belt culture even before he begins his train ride into the South.

It is in the narrative's representation of the key figures of rural African-American culture—nothing less than archetypes of a fading antebellum world that take him deepest into his racial past—that the disjunctions of the Ex-Coloured Man's ethnographic project are most keen. As always, his intentions bifurcate between possibilities. Because they derive from Johnson's own biographical memories, which would be repeated in the first *Book of Ameri-*

can Negro Spirituals, the narrator's portraits of the preacher John Brown and the song leader Singing Johnson may be taken at face value as a legitimate honoring of the roots of African-American culture. By the same token, John Brown and Singing Johnson are also cultural resources that Johnson himself "mined"—to the extent, one might even say, that like his narrator he could not easily draw a line between helping his people and distinguishing himself as an artist. The verbal arts of John Brown would form the basis for Johnson's experimental verse in *God's Trombones* (his "primitive poetry" will be considered in that connection alongside Hurston's Lovelace sermon in chapter 2). A more complex figure in Johnson's circuitous self-representation, Singing Johnson was the embodiment of those "Black and Unknown Bards," as Johnson would call them in his famous poem of that title, who created the great body of the spirituals—the anonymous singers who, along with the community worshipping around them, forged a great Afro-Christian musical literature and functioned in a manner reminiscent of their ancestral African bards to bring history into the living present.

As in his tribute to the arts of leadership displayed by the black preacher, where he followed the lead of Du Bois, Johnson's portrait of Singing Johnson reiterated central elements of *The Souls of Black Folk*. Once again, however, the Ex-Coloured Man's narrative quickly swerves into ethical incoherence when he himself is compared to the objects of his celebration. Like the bards honored by Du Bois as the spiritual source of the "faith of the fathers," Singing Johnson is essentially a kind of historian. His skills at leading a congregation in song, perfectly supporting the message of the minister with his music and committing to memory hundreds of spirituals, make him the reservoir of African-American culture and a link to an African past, a feature even more pronounced in the first *Book of American Negro Spirituals*, where Johnson links the spirituals to African call-and-response forms. Singing Johnson, however, has precisely what the narrator lacks: ancestral memory and racial history. He is not presented as the originator of particular songs but rather as an emblem of the spirituals' creators, who may have been strong individual personalities but were nonetheless immersed in the communal act of creation. Their anonymity, that is to say, is a sign of both historical community and the precious survival of cultural forms throughout the duress of slavery. The narrator's anonymity, on the other hand, is negative: it is a sign of historical discontinuity and the renunciation of cultural forms. Along one route lies the recovery of the unknown and the anonymous—the true spirituals that never get written down (as Hurston would contend), the greatest flights of improvisation that never get recorded (as Ralph Ellison would argue in his provocative essay on Charlie Christian). The mythos of untraceable origins and unwritten—or rather, continually "rewritten"— texts puts a premium on remembering, on acts of consciousness that ground the racial nation and tie together its generations throughout the African diaspora. Along the route followed by the Ex-Coloured Man, however, lies cultural forgetting, the disintegration of racial consciousness.

Among the many scenes from *The Souls of Black Folk* rewritten in Johnson's novel, in fact, perhaps none is so important as the scene from "Of the Coming of John," Du Bois's one piece of fiction in the book and a work in which he figuratively examined his own divided cultural sensibility. When the character John returns to Georgia after his long sojourn in the North, his welcome at the Baptist Church is ruined by his brusque manner and by his dismissal, during his short speech on education, of the African-American church as an antiquated institution. John's rebuke from a church elder is a powerful sketch of the quality of faith that Du Bois located in the slave generation: "He seized the

Bible with his rough, huge hands; twice he raised it inarticulate, and then fairly burst into words, with rude and awful eloquence. He quivered, swayed, and bent; then rose aloft in perfect majesty, till the people moaned and wept, wailed and shouted, and a wild shrieking arose from the corners where all the pent-up feeling of the hour gathered itself and rushed into the air. John never knew clearly what the old man said; he only felt himself held up to scorn and scathing denunciation for trampling on the true Religion, and he realized with amazement that all unknowingly he had put rough, rude hands on something this little world held sacred." The vice in which John is caught, underscored by his humming of Wagner's "Song of the Bride" at the point of his ambiguous death by lynching or suicide, was nothing less than the vice of divided identity in which Du Bois himself and later Johnson were caught: how to balance the acquisition of white, European cultural forms against the preserved beliefs and cultural patterns of black America that had originated in slavery or in Africa. John is denounced by the embodiment of the preacher as Du Bois defined him in "Of the Faith of the Fathers," a combined tyrant, judge, and seer; the Ex-Coloured Man's own self-denunciation appears at the end of the novel, but it is implicit as well in his portraits of John Brown and Singing Johnson, representatives of the sacred world that he forsakes. In this respect, his renunciation of African-American culture—not just his decision not to appropriate it to his own ends, as Johnson himself would, but his decision to erase it from consciousness altogether—combines the worst traits of middle-class rejection of slave culture and a deliberate choice not to build the race itself. When he decides to pass, the Ex-Coloured Man enacts both the physical and the semiotic destruction of a world in which color and language bear the meaning of ancestry.

In *Along This Way*, Johnson recalled his three months of teaching in rural Georgia in terms not entirely unlike his narrator's. He too took something of an ethnological perspective, studying the rural folk "with a sympathetic objectivity, as though they were something apart." But he also recognized, he wrote in retrospect, that "they were me, and I was they; that a force stronger than blood made us one," and that in the capacity of the folk to survive, labor, and raise families lay their great strength. Johnson's location of what he carefully called the "basic material of race building" in the "deep-bosomed" fertility of black women—their color, gayety, laughter, song, and undulating movement, "a heritage from the African jungle," as he wrote—may at first glance seem marred by a gendered exoticism. Yet he specifically contrasted the beautiful black woman of the folk to "her sallow, songless, lipless, hipless, tired-looking, tired-moving white sister"—just the sort of white beauty, he said, that was constantly held up to blacks as an ideal, just the sort of white beauty, indeed, that the Ex-Coloured Man marries and chooses to bear his children, who will know nothing of their African-American past.

It is a biographical coincidence that Singing Johnson's name echoes that of James Weldon Johnson, yet it is not farfetched to say that Johnson took this occasion to underscore his own potential declension from the faith of the fathers. Because virtually the same passages about Singing Johnson appear in Johnson's later prefaces, one must conclude that his admiration for the deep historical heritage of African-American preaching and singing is utterly sincere—a deliberate counterpoint to the foolish caricatures of the black preacher common in much minstrelsy and to the remaining detractors of the black spirituals as legitimate art. Yet the admiring, historically vibrant portrait of the "big meeting" at which John Brown and Singing Johnson hold center stage crumbles in the face of the narrator's own epistemological and moral confusion. First, he persuasively argues that a true rendition of the spirituals produces "one of the most thrilling emotions which the human heart may experience." "I sat often with the tears rolling down my cheeks and my heart melted within me," reports the narrator. Within two paragraphs and a few hours, however, he complains that his host, a rural black schoolteacher, is "too much in earnest over the race question." If the mass of Negroes took the future as seriously as their leaders and failed to exercise a slight sense of humor, he remarks, "the race would be in no mental condition to sustain the terrible pressure which it undergoes." This takes the great tradition of African-American humor, certainly a source of resistance and sustenance, and twists it in a painful direction. In the narrator's supercilious, disoriented account, the two realms of experience bear no relation to one another—the compelling beauty of "Go Down, Moses" having virtually nothing to do with the "terrible pressure" of the "race question."

We are left to wonder whether such misunderstanding and condescension are inherent in the protagonist's character or have been woven into the mask of self-justification that his retrospective narrative requires. In either case, the jarring juxtaposition of sentiments provides a perfect entry to the lynching scene that follows, which begins with the Ex-Coloured Man, like a dedicated ethnographer in from the field, "looking over [his] notes and jotting down some ideas which were still fresh in [his] mind." In the midst of his musings, a vague alarm and turmoil catches his attention; at length he is swept up into the frightening chaos of a lynching, not as a potential victim but as a witness whose very identity lies in what he sees and how he allows himself to be seen. The narrator has already told us that in traveling about rural Georgia he "was sometimes amused on arriving at some little railroad-station town to be taken for and treated as a white man." This ruse anticipates his final decision to claim neither race: "Let the world take me for what it would." But if he disabuses the townspeople in most instances, he fails to do so at the moment—or at least in the aftermath of the moment—when it matters most, the witnessed lynching: "Perhaps what bravery I exercised in going out," he woodenly admits, "was due to the fact that I felt sure my identity as a coloured man had not yet become known in the town."

The lynching scene is all the more provocative for having been inspired by an incident in Johnson's own life in 1900. Walking in Jacksonville with a female journalist who was legally black but visibly white, he was arrested by military police on the charge of simply being with a white woman. Because Johnson knew well enough to cooperate fully, thus calming the hostilities of the small mob who gathered as he and his friend were seized, and because he also knew the provost marshall before whom he would be brought, the "melodrama that might have been tragedy," as he later described it, had a simple resolution. For months, however, it produced in Johnson recurrent nightmares of what could have happened—"the nightmare of a struggle with a band of murderous, bloodthirsty men in khaki, with loaded rifles and fixed bayonets." It would take some twenty years and his work for the NAACP on behalf of civil rights and antilynching legislation, Johnson later wrote, to liberate himself "completely from this horror complex." In the actual incident, the "black" woman, no doubt protected by her gender, got away with berating the embarrassed marshall and condemning "the sins of his fathers and his fathers' fathers" as responsible for the nearly catastrophic confusion—but responsible as well for the grotesque color line that defined Johnson's mere acquaintance with a seemingly "white" woman as a race crime. In the novel, Johnson rewrote the parts, transferring the ironies of the woman's whiteness to the narrator himself, who, far from protesting the violent outburst of race hate, watches from a ghostly distance the actualization of Johnson's nightmare before electing to retreat into the genealogical color safety provided for him by the sins of his fathers' fathers. The Ex-Coloured

Man cannot be liberated from the "horror complex" of the lynching, but for different reason. He is transfixed by the spectacle itself and remains "powerless to take [his] eyes from what [he] did not want to see"—both the racial carnage before him and his divided common heritage in it.

The spectatorship that marks the protagonist's relation to his blackness throughout the book, from the moment he first views himself in the mirror as an uncanny white Negro boy, rises to a wrenching height in this scene, where he stands both on and off stage, on both sides of the color line. His participation in the scene is infused with passivity but at the same time charged with tremulous excitement, just as the regimentation of the mob is laced with outbursts of diabolical frenzy. Terror and fascination are mixed in Johnson's masterly prose, which renders the lynching in brutal detail while simultaneously keeping our attention on the qualities of the narrator's own language—his absorption in the staged spectacle, his mesmerism by the stoic precision of racism acted out, his utter ambivalence toward the anonymous victim. "Have you ever witnessed the transformation of human beings into savage beasts?" the narrator asks, almost quizzically. Within two sentences, in fact, the exact location of the bestial has shifted in the narrator's perspective to his description of the lynching victim: "There he stood, a man only in form and stature, every sign of degeneracy stamped upon his countenance. His eyes were dull and vacant, indicating not a single ray of thought. . . . He was too stunned and stupefied even to tremble." "As weak as a man who has lost blood," the narrator drags himself from the scene, packs his bags, boards the northbound train, and becomes a white man, losing his own black blood as surely as the victim he has just seen burned to death. The unnamed lynching victim is the unnamed narrator's inverted double, his mirror image, for it is in the act of witnessing that he most becomes an "ex-coloured man," inadvertently as savage a spectator as the others who flock to the public ritual. Disclaiming the "label of inferiority pasted across [his] forehead" that admission of his racial mix would entail and expressing shame at identification with people who could be "treated worse than animals," the narrator becomes the man whose story we are reading—a man who has "never really been a Negro," as he finally admits, but "only a privileged spectator of their inner life."

The terror of the lynching arises in part from the fact that we never discover what crime the man is held to have committed. Given its sources in Johnson's own experience, however, one is not wrong to assume a specious charge of "rape" and to bear in mind Johnson's summation of his own near-lynching: "In the core of the heart of the American race problem the sex factor is rooted." One version of Johnson's judgment about America's racial rape complex appears in his haunting poem "The White Witch," in which the white woman is portrayed as an evil temptress behind whose smiling lips "the spirit of a vampire lies." The poem aroused great controversy for its satire of white sexual pathology, but nothing bears out his thesis more strongly than the scalding irony of the Ex-Coloured Man's choice not just to pass but to marry white and father white children. What the narrator refers to as the secret "practical joke" of his passing into white culture, coyly infecting its purity with his hidden black blood, is a pathetic mask for his abnegation. Both the opening stance of Poe-like confidence man and the mock-sober "publisher's" preface citing the "unascertainable number" of blacks passing for white (most likely written by Johnson himself) are drained away in Johnson's archly satiric reversal of the tragic mulatto romance that concludes the narrator's confession. As though to eradicate blackness altogether he marries a woman who is a burlesque of whiteness—"the most dazzlingly white thing I had ever seen," as he says—and a classical pianist, her fragile body, delicate beauty, and fine voice the perfect vessel of high European culture. Their love is sealed when the Ex-Coloured Man resolves Chopin's Thirteenth Nocturne on a major triad—not the minor it requires, and something far from the "barbaric harmonies" and "audacious resolutions" of his ragtime days—thus silencing the minor key of his black life for good and consigning to oblivion his music manuscripts, "the only tangible remnants of a vanished dream, a dead ambition, a sacrificed talent."

· · ·

"The Southern whites are in many respects a great people. Looked at from a certain point of view, they are picturesque. If one will put oneself in a romantic frame of mind, one can admire their notions of chivalry and bravery and justice." Thus remarks the narrator in the immediate aftermath of the lynching. He goes on, of course, to say that a people capable of such race brutality is not living in the present age but rather harks back to a world replete with "the bloody deeds of pirates and the fierce brutality of vikings." The narrator's characteristically double-edged prose, which allows him to ridicule neo-Confederate traditions of masculine heroism while at the same time himself luxuriating in detached, philosophical judgment, is the remark of a white man, not a black man in the age of Jim Crow. From "a certain point of view" lynching is barbarous, savage; from "a certain point of view," African-American culture is degraded, inferior. The lynching victim's "blackened bones, charred fragments sifting down through coils of chain; and the smell of burnt flesh" shock the protagonist, even prompt him to pen a miniature essay on southern handling of the "Negro question" and the Atlanta riot—but he sees and feels them from behind a protective mask of whiteness.

Perspective is everything in this novel, and the narrator's moral cowardice lies not in his failure to go to the aid of the lynched man, which would have been futile, or even publicly to declare himself black, which would accomplish little. Rather, his shame and disgrace lie in the choice he makes to expunge his racial heritage, to forsake race-building not just in his procreation but more importantly in his artistic and scholarly creation. Through the medium of his narrator's privileged point of observation, Johnson matched the panoramic spectacle of the "big meeting," its vibrant re-creation of the ancestral sources of living black culture, to the spectacle of the lynching, its ritual enactment of the doctrine of white supremacy. In the "spectacular" nature of the lynching, Johnson not only played on real-life models but also brought into view how iconographic lynching spectacles in both the real world and the world of art or literature could help to drive African Americans first into economic and political submission and next into cultural oblivion. Of course Johnson asked his readers what choice they might make if faced with the opportunity to become "ex-coloured" people. But he also asked on the one hand how many visibly black people might already have become "ex-coloured" in their rejection of African-American culture, and on the other how many whites had no notion at all of the culture that they routinely condemned or sought to destroy.

Johnson asked questions, that is to say, that have remained remarkably alive, uncomfortably pertinent over the course of the twentieth century. What the narrator considers the "joke" played on his white audience by his confessional tale depends on activating their horror at discovering that a "colored" man has passed unknown into their midst, married their white daughter, contaminated the blood of their grandchildren—in short, discovering that a black man has acted out a rank parody of their stereotypical racial nightmare. (According to one estimate, some ten to twenty-five thousand men and women passed yearly between 1900 and 1910, the uncertainty of the census obviously a sign of the phenomenon itself.) But the dismaying and tragic pressure of his joke runs in the other direction as well, for it is black culture, not white, that is destroyed by the Ex-Coloured Man's choice. Blacks could be lynched by more genteel means than rope and fagot, Joel Williamson has observed of the nadir; they could be lynched by account books and by scholarly histories that paved the way for reunion politics. They could be lynched by mulattoes, such as Charles Carroll and William Hannibal Thomas, who pandered to white supremacy by writing racist diatribes. And they could be lynched as well by those, like the Ex-Coloured Man, who expunge their color and their history in a fantasia of whiteness. The blackened, charred bones that linger momentarily in the protagonist's memory of the lynching are, in effect, his own bones, the framework and sinew of the culture that he has forsaken.

James Weldon Johnson, fortunately, did no such thing. W. S. Scarborough had in 1899 challenged the black novelist to give up vaudeville and minstrelsy, to ignore the temptation, like that of Esau, "to sell his birthright for a mess of pottage" and write instead on serious African-American themes. Whether or not Johnson had Scarborough's essay in mind when he reworked the biblical passage into his protagonist's last feeble moment of self-awareness, he himself only tested the betrayal of race building in order to engage in race building. Writing most of his novel in Venezuela, a nation whose racial fluidity made the color line of the United States all the more stark, Johnson could stand outside the racial dilemma just long enough to imagine an alternative—as well as the moral burden and cultural loss it would entail. The protagonist's narrative is a masterly catalogue of evasions and half-truths surrounding brilliant exercises in African-American cultural preservation—the account of ragtime, the signifying recapitulations of Douglass, Washington, and Du Bois, most of all the portraits of John Brown and Singing Johnson. What *The Autobiography of an Ex-Coloured Man* demonstrates is the painful degree to which racial violence and fear, the alluring forces of assimilation to the ideals of dominant culture, and the historical erosion of memory can together threaten a minority culture. African-American culture as it was represented in the spirituals, as in folklore, was paradoxically thriving and dying at the same time when Johnson wrote. Recorded and collected in significant quantities, it had nonetheless become scholarly, arranged, commercialized: as Hurston might have said, it was at the point of becoming "neo-slave culture," if it was not being altogether suppressed or lost. In this novel that reflected on work behind him as a popular lyricist and work to come as an advocate of the spirituals, Johnson stood not quite on the color line, as did his passing alter ego, but on the culture line. He represented the act of African-American cultural recovery and preservation in the face of its greatest costs and risks; and in doing so he paid his greatest tribute to the cultural heritage of the South and that of the nation, which, consciously or not, was itself becoming increasingly black, increasingly southern.

TWO

"The Drum with the Man Skin":
Jonah's Gourd Vine

The spirituals included in volumes such as James Weldon and Rosamond Johnson's first and second *Book of American Negro Spirituals* and the many comparable collections frequently showed pronounced variations resulting not simply from the difficulty of transcription or from historical erosion but rather from the fact that spirituals, in their origins, were fundamentally a communal, improvisatory art. What survives in written, published form depends to some degree upon chance, and the "text" may at that point once again become an occasion for further invention in which communal effort and individual performance are intertwined. Upon a given framework of chord changes, melodic line, and lyric theme, countless variations were created and lost before the late nineteenth century and since, and those elements of early modern black arts that derived from folk culture owe a great deal to an expressive form, both in songs and folktales, that in some respects is antithetical to the notion of a fixed, regulated text. In their landmark 1926 collection, *Blues: An Anthology*, W. C. Handy and Abbe Niles traced Handy's art to African-American worship, where the preacher's lining out of a hymn and the congregation's response formed a dialectic. After the preacher had lined out a portion of the song in his own shout or wail, which was characteristically full of blue notes (a source of Handy's early composition, he recalled), the congregation would adapt the example to their own creative purposes: "From every note each singer would start on a vocal journey of his own, wandering in strange pentatonic figures, but returning together at the proper moment to the next note of the melody. If one had succeeded in attracting attention by an exceptional note or a striking rhythmic figure, a dozen others would attempt, starting from the next note, to outdo him. To an unaccustomed listener close at hand, the result would be chaos, but at a distance the sounds merged into a strange and moving harmony."

Niles's description of Handy's apprenticeship is striking on several counts. It recapitulates the wealth of commentary that was available, beginning with the earliest studies of slave spirituals and work songs, about the divergence of black American music from the tempered scale and harmonic structure of most European, Protestant music; it indicates a vocal confluence between preaching and singing that elides the registers of speech and music, a central feature of African-American aesthetics; and its description of the call-and-response format underlines the interaction between community and individual performance in black folk culture as it was frequently recorded and then re-created in literary form by Zora Neale Hurston. Indeed, all these elements are bound together in Hurston's most significant writing, which always occupies the abraded border terrain between the oral and the written, between the recorded and the re-created. Unlike Johnson, who highly valued African-American folk culture but argued for its transfiguration into more "sophisticated" forms, Hurston, as we have seen, hyperidealized vernacular, asserting in her famous 1934 essay "Spirituals and Neo-Spirituals" that there never had been a legitimate presentation of "genuine Negro spirituals to any audience anywhere." The true songs, like the true folktales, she said, were "being made and forgotten every day." By the same token, of course, Hurston's career was founded on the premise that the vernacular could be translated, so to speak, into disseminated form—in ethnographic collections, in critical essays, and in fiction.

For this reason, the liminality of her own authorial and professional voice bears an important resemblance to the liminality of her characters' voices—whether those of anthropological subject-informants or fictive protagonists—for all of them frequently inhabit the blurred grounds between folklore and fiction, music and voice. The undervalued "Spirituals and Neo-Spirituals" is most often cited for its rather idiosyncratic elevation of vernacular improvisation in the spirituals. Much of the essay, however, is devoted to Hurston's extremely acute analysis of the intersection between black song and sermonic form, to the "tonal semantics" (to borrow Geneva Smitherman's modern phrase) that lie at the heart of black American expressivity as it was nurtured in the Afro-Christian church and that appear as a primary aesthetic device in her first novel, *Jonah's Gourd Vine* (1936). Perhaps the single most revealing essay in the early theorizing of African-American vernacular culture—leaving aside the more magisterial thesis put forward by Du Bois in *The Souls of Black Folk*—"Spirituals and Neo-Spirituals" is an important gloss on the long-standing debate over dialect verse, the rise of blues and gospel, and the question of community leadership in its relationship to aesthetics—a relationship that is attenuated at best in the Euro-American tradition but can be shown to be central to the African-American tradition.

"As bard, physician, judge, and priest . . . rose the Negro preacher, and under him the first Afro-American institution, the

Negro church," wrote Du Bois of the black preacher, in addition styling him "a leader, a politician, an orator, a 'boss,' an intriguer, [and] an idealist." Hurston's early work did not so thoroughly rewrite *The Souls of Black Folk* as had Johnson's *Autobiography of an Ex-Coloured Man*, though her seminal essays for Nancy Cunard's *Negro: An Anthology* (although the essays were written in 1930, the anthology was published in 1934) and *Jonah's Gourd Vine* go a long way toward developing in theoretical detail Du Bois's central concerns in "Of the Faith of the Fathers": "the Preacher, the Music, and the Frenzy." Although he was modeled in telling ways on Hurston's own father, the preacher John Pearson in her first novel embodied most of the traits of cultural leadership that Du Bois had ennumerated, even as he glaringly displayed the faults and sins apparent in the autobiographical figure. More importantly, however, John Pearson became the vehicle for Hurston's testing of the very medium of African-American culture. His is the voice whose "liquefying of words," as she called it, linked sermon to music to communal response; the voice whose tale telling yoked improvisation to a complex allegorical structure, making biblical scripture potently alive with parabolic significance for the African diaspora and the delivery from bondage; the voice whose cadences continually rewrote the languages of resistance and striving carried out of slavery into a modern idiom— what Hurston would refer to in *Their Eyes Were Watching God* (1937) as "words walking without masters; walking altogether like harmony in a song." What is more, it is a voice whose combined power and ambiguity of intention allowed Hurston to find and explore her own voice as an African-American author.

In order to gauge these various interpenetrating elements of vocality that Hurston put at the core of both her ethnographic and fictive work, I will concentrate on the origins of John Pearson's career, Hurston's theory of sermonic language, and the sermon of the Reverend C. C. Lovelace. The Lovelace sermon was first transcribed by Hurston in Eau Gallie, Florida, in 1929, then published along with "Spirituals and Neo-Spirituals" in Cunard's *Negro*, and finally inserted into the text of *Jonah's Gourd Vine* in the mouth of John Pearson when, in a grand sermon, he attempts to redeem himself in the eyes of his congregation, diverting their attention from his marital infidelities and moral weaknesses. Although some readers have lamented that Hurston stretched the plot of her novel incongruously to provide an occasion to display the Lovelace sermon in the mouth of John Pearson, my focus here will be less on the novel's story line and characterizations than on the intersection of its folk and narrative registers. Unlike *Their Eyes Were Watching God*, for example, in which those registers are seamlessly woven together in Hurston's mature narrative discourse—the voices of author and character carefully merged, embedding African-American inflections and figures into a "speaking" text—*Jonah's Gourd Vine* is patently experimental, even jagged in its composition. Virtually stylized moments seem deliberately provided in the novel for Hurston to examine black "talk" (signifying), the issue of African retentions, altiloquent figures of speech, the train as African-American metaphor, the work song as a folk source, and most of all, of course, the sermon as performative art. Indeed, the very stylization of these moments is the source of their meaning; they lay bare the process of integration by which Hurston rehearsed the preservation of slave culture in the twentieth century and reconstructed the notion of the novel in an African-American cultural context. Like Johnson in *The Autobiography of an Ex-Coloured Man*, she searched into the survivals of slave culture for the materials of a modern black culture that would properly preserve and extend racial consciousness rather than see it eroded, even erased, by white culture; and like him, she wrote a novel that was principally a metacommentary on novelization. But wherever Johnson was ambivalent or conservative, Hurston was typically daring and unreserved in her indulgent celebration of folk culture as the only undiluted voice of black America.

. . .

Hurston's caustic signifying on Johnson in *Dust Tracks on a Road*—that he had for years been "passing for colored"—hardly gives an adequate indication of the admiration she held for him and his work. As suggested in chapter 1, her comic critique provides one way to read her pronounced divergence from him on the issue of the spirituals and "authentic" African-American vocality. For the same reason, it may be read as a reflection of her sincere appraisal not of his aesthetic intentions but of his aesthetic achievement. In the wake of a misinformed review of *Jonah's Gourd Vine*, Hurston complained to Johnson that the reviewer was unwilling to recognize that a Negro preacher like John Pearson "could have so much poetry in him" and failed to understand that the preacher, in order to hold his charge, had to be an "artist": "He must be both a poet and an actor of a very high order, and then he must have the voice and figure. [The reviewer] does not realize or is unwilling to admit that the light that shone from *God's Trombones* was handed to you, as was the sermon to me in *Jonah's Gourd Vine*." As in her theory of the spirituals, Hurston suggested that what went unrecorded was perhaps even more significant: "There are hundreds of preachers who are equalling that sermon weekly."

Hurston's entire characterization of the preacher's leadership and art bears closer examination, but her further remark to Johnson that the two of them "seem to be the only ones even among Negroes who recognize the barbaric poetry in their sermons" elides a profound difference between their mutual understandings and uses of that language (as well as conveniently setting aside other writers and ethnographers who argued for the same importance of the African-American sermon). A further, rather more complicated difference is also elided in Hurston's assertion that both the poetry of *God's Trombones* and the Lovelace sermon were "handed" to the two authors. Johnson, as indicated in chapter 1, based the first of his poems, "The Creation," on a Kansas City preacher who cast aside his formal text in favor of the oratorical vernacular. In all the poems of *God's Trombones*, Johnson composed verse rooted in that experience but hardly replicating it, building in subsequent poems of the sequence on the experience of collecting and analyzing the spirituals for his two published volumes. Hurston, on the other hand, seems virtually to have reproduced the substance of Lovelace's sermon for her Cunard essay, casting it into verse form but preserving its language and cadence, then incorporating it bodily into *Jonah's Gourd Vine*. Her choice of form is significant in both instances, as is, even more obviously, her decision to move the work from one genre to another. In addition, the Lovelace sermon is distinctly more complex in figure and rhetoric than most of the sermons of the period that were being published in journals such as the *Southern Workman* or issued on the race records that flooded the market in the 1920s and 1930s, and the degree of Hurston's intervention may perhaps be a more serious issue than she herself let on. First, however, one can look at Johnson's sermonic verse and his theory of dialect as a way of estimating Hurston's pointed divergence from his model. Dialect writing and the folk sources of its intonations contained within it African sounds propelled into a unique black American vernacular that, as Hurston and Johnson both saw clearly, was to remain a kind of crossroads of cultural languages. As in the case of the spirituals, however, the nuanced difference in their views of dialect is more telling than their points of agreement. On the face of it (although we do not have the original preacher's sermon for comparison), Johnson's is the more composed, the more conventional aesthetic work, demonstrating, as in *his* theory of the spirituals, a "development" of vernacular materials into a more "cultivated," authorial form. Nevertheless, because *God's Trombones* is noticeably less interesting as sermonic language and as poetry, it raises pressing questions about idiom and about the context of publication by which we judge the value of cultural works.

"The old-time Negro preacher is rapidly passing," Johnson writes in his preface to *God's Trombones*, "I have here tried sincerely to fix something of him." The verses of *God's Trombones*, as this passage suggests, are a powerful memorial tribute, a display in Johnson's rather stately language of seven of the major biblical themes of the African-American sermon. His well-known renunciation of dialect (already spelled out in the preface to the *Book of American Negro Poetry* several years earlier and then reiterated in *God's Trombones*) hinges on his view that dialect had typically been the medium of picturesque racism—plantation romance and "darky" humor—even for the black writer. Johnson himself had composed traditional dialect poems—"jingles and croons," as he called them—but in later editions of his own poetry he reprinted such verse as "Ma Lady's Lips Am Like de Honey" and "Brer Rabbit, You's de Cutes' of 'Em All" primarily as archaic data that bore out his own theory. On the other hand, in the 1931 edition of the poetry anthology and in his preface to Sterling Brown's *Southern Road* a year later, Johnson somewhat revised his opinion, allowing that Brown and Langston Hughes had transcended minstrelsy and discovered in dialect the "common, racy, living, authentic speech of the Negro." Such exceptions, however, proved the rule that black authors should, in Johnson's words, seek to "express the racial spirit by symbols from within rather than symbols from without—such as the mere mutilation of

English spelling and pronunciation." In *God's Trombones*, then, Johnson sought to re-create the black preacher's "tone pictures," as he called them in describing the folk preacher John Brown in *The Autobiography of an Ex-Coloured Man*; but he did so without recourse to textual markings that would replace conventional dialect with the vernacular signs of blackness and without actualizing a number of the features he had so precisely theorized in his preface. In avoiding the risks of dialect, Johnson at the same time sacrificed its strengths, which are considerable though not simple to specify—or, more accurately, to "hear."

Charles Chesnutt once complained in a letter to Walter Hines Page that it was a "despairing task" to write dialect. The problem was not just orthographic but theoretical. Echoing an increasing tradition of fieldwork, Chesnutt argued that "there is no such thing as a Negro dialect. . . . what we call by that name is the attempt to express, with such a degree of phonetic correctness as to suggest the sound, English pronounced as an ignorant old southern Negro would be supposed to speak it, and at the same time to preserve a sufficient approximation to the correct spelling to make it easy reading." Chesnutt's discomforting detachment from the rural southern folk does not discredit the evaluative importance of his views or his own effective use of dialect for ideological purpose in *The Conjure Woman* (1899) and elsewhere. Moreover, Chesnutt's argument, which posited a black vernacular but said it could not be accurately cast into readable print, would appear to invert the complaint voiced by Howard Odum and Guy Johnson in their important collection of black folksongs, *The Negro and His Songs* (1925), that dialect was hard to record because "there is no regular usage for any word in the Negro's vocabulary," or Newbell Puckett's degrading judgment that the "altiloquent speech" of blacks, satirized in grotesque exaggeration by minstrelsy, showed that "the Negro is constantly being lost in a labyrinth of jaw-breaking words full of sound and fury but signifying nothing." "Signifying nothing," however, might turn out to be a revealing characterization: African-American dialect, in high culture no less than in folk culture, was in a constant condition of signifying on the linguistic power of the masters, appropriating and depleting that power, at least provisionally, by subverting its authority and thus reducing it to "nothing."

Dialect, as Chesnutt saw, was complex semantically and politically, as the significant turn-of-the-century debate about it reveals. An anonymous writer for the *Atlantic Monthly* in 1891, arguing that the language of former slaves and their descendants was a mystified jumble of misunderstood English, inadvertently located the crucial double-terrain of ethnic vernacular when he designated dialect as a language of "word-shadows." African-American dialect, the author argued, is composed of "the shadows cast by words from fairly educated lips into the minds of almost totally ignorant people," the light of civilization thrown into the "dusky realm" of savagery producing "something queer, fanciful, and awkward," a new language it must employ "since it has lost the tongue of its own people." The author goes on to list many examples of highly figurative transformations in black English— for example, a giant is a "high-jinted man"; to keep down grass is to "fight wid Gen'al Green"; to join a church is to "put on a shine-line gyarment"—of the very sort Hurston would later say were characteristic of the "adornment" and "angularity" of black speech. Although his argument is a tissue of commonplace racist assumptions of the post–Reconstruction era, the *Atlantic* author's essay offers important clues to the function of dialect. Because he understood dialect to mean not just accent or intonation but also figurative diction, the writer was somewhat closer than most of his contemporaries to recognizing that African-American language represented a creative as well as a necessary merger, over a number of generations, of native linguistic survivals and the language of Euro-Americans, assimilated in oral forms.

When it was defined in relation to a dominant culture, dialect might therefore function as an index of the power of signs to exclude and oppress; but it might for that same reason indicate a powerful mode of cultural self-determination and self-preservation. As Henry Louis Gates, Jr., has argued, dialect can turn the "metaphor against its master." Located between the two poles of white English and an African language "lost in some mythical linguistic kingdom now irrecoverable," black dialect can be read as the only surviving key to that unknown tongue. Moreover, Gates's view that successful dialect writing is fundamentally musical and approaches the metaphoric richness of black spirituals—a level that dialect poetry or prose has, however, seldom reached, most obviously in the early modern generation in the cases of Hurston and Brown—underlines the necessity that dialect be understood to include the semantic plenitude and singularity of folk speech as well as its oral legends, its material and psychological space, and the implied ancestral sources of its language and beliefs. The "word-shadows" of black dialect may be perceived by whites as a distorted version of correct English or a potentially destructive presence within the master's culture and thus subject to mockery and exorcism through the degrading parody of minstrel stereotypes. In addition, however, dialect must be seen as a signifying alternative, another cultural language historically related to white English while transfiguring it as well.

Whereas ethnologists were prone to characterizing black language as the idiom of a social and cultural world that failed to measure up to civilized standards, there was the counterpossibility, exploited notably by Chesnutt and again more dramatically by Hurston, that black language was also the idiom of a secret world kept out of range to the middle-class mind, much as the coded languages of slavery had been deliberately kept out of the range of the masters. To borrow Ralph Ellison's powerful metaphor, it was a language that spoke on "lower frequencies." Dissembling its communications within a culturally distinct, necessarily private communal language, dialect, like the intonations of the spirituals, may be seen to be governed by hidden semantic constructions and grounded in a signifying response to white culture dating from the origins of slavery. Insofar as it reconstructed slave culture, dialect was both a salvaged speech that pays tribute to those who have gone before and an index of what has been kept alive in the evolving cultural memory of song, folktale, and everyday language. Far from being the obvious sign of regression or the inadequate comprehension of civilized cultural forms, dialect might be the linguistic tool best able to show that the bondage of language could also be liberating.

In this respect in particular dialect bears an important relation to the African-American spirituals. For whites' complaints about the ineffability of black dialect, which led in turn to the grotesque caricatures of minstrelsy and some plantation romance, repeated comparable observations by musicologists, as we have seen in chapter 1, that the intonations of the black spiritual were difficult to transcribe. The opinion of Thomas Fenner, the white arranger of the spirituals sung and published by Hampton Institute, was characteristic: "Another obstacle to [the music's] rendering is the fact that tones are frequently employed which we have no musical characters to represent. . . . These tones are variable in pitch, ranging through an entire interval on different occasions, depending on the inspiration of the singer." As Hurston and others complained, however, the "purification" of African-American spirituals by touring choirs and concert performers eliminated or reconfigured any residual elements of African folk art and the unique sounds forged in slave culture when those characteristic tonalities and rhythms were made to conform more closely to European standards. F. G. Rathbun, writing of Hampton Institute's programs in the *Southern Workman* in 1893, summed up the paradox of the educational process in this way: "After a contact with our sight singing teacher, our English teacher and teacher of elocution, something is missing from these songs, and this goes on as long as the student remains here. Corrected pronunciation and corrected singing make the difference. It is very difficult to teach an educated colored youth to render these songs in the old time way."

In a signifying reversal of the denigration of black dialect as a mere "shadow" of traditional English, Hurston and other early celebrants of African-American language sought to value and preserve the sounds of slave culture threatened with extinction by forced adherence to white educational and artistic standards. As Fenner's caveat suggested, the convergence of musicality and meaning in African-American speech meant that the recorded sign, not the act of signification, would be the "shadow," the inadequate container for a meaning that slid away in the act of performance. The political level of circumspection in black language that slavery entailed has survived on through the twentieth century in the deeply musical vernacular forms of speech, language games, signifying, and sermonizing analyzed by Geneva Smitherman, Claudia Mitchell-Kernan, Roger Abrahams, and others. The principal strategies of indirection that ethnomusicologists have found to be characteristic of African and African-American music in this way strengthen the tight fusion of tonal and semantic qualities in black vernacular language. Increasingly in the early twentieth century, black writers, throwing off the post–Reconstruction anxiety about slave culture and seeking to re-create ancestral traditions, recognized that the elaborate metaphoricity and what seemed the unfixed character of African-American language could be construed positively—as a linguistic medium whose fluidity and capacity for improvisation was akin to the development of improvisatory arts in black vocal and instrumental music.

It is just here that Hurston diverged from and improved the astute theorizing of Johnson. Even so, she seems, in fact, to have traded on some of the key observations that Johnson made in his preface to *God's Trombones*. Like her, he rightly put oratory and acting on the same plane in the preacher's performance, noting that the biblical text could sometimes serve as a mere starting point for a sermonic flight; he underlined the centrality of rhythm and intonation in the sermon, placing particular emphasis on the appearance of breathing as a part of the expression and suggesting that the "sense of sound" itself was of such overriding importance that he had seen congregations "moved to ecstasy by the rhythmic intoning of sheer incoherencies"; and he contended that the preacher's language was a "fusion of Negro idioms with Bible English," in which there likely resided "some kinship with the innate grandiloquence of [the] old African tongues." All of these points reappear in transfigured form in "Spirituals and Neo-Spirituals" and *Jonah's Gourd Vine*, but in each case Hurston seems to have articulated better what is specifically African-American in these elements and to have found their natural equivalent in her own rendition of the Lovelace sermon.

In Johnson's taped recordings of *God's Trombones*, the relative formality and stateliness is evident in his own vocal "intonation," which, though Carl Van Vechten complimented its emotive power and Johnson's expert delivery, seems rather flat. His elevated tones and extended syllabic phrasing verge at times on a kind of singsong that seems distant from the experience of the Kansas City preacher that must have been in the back of Johnson's mind (and distant as well from the better recorded sermons of the same or later years). The problem seems to lie less in Johnson's voice, however, than in his verse. S. P. Fullinwider's contention that *God's Trombones* is "anthropology, not creativity" is not quite right, nor is Jean Wagner's kinder and more useful judgment that it is a kind of "stylized folklore." The black folk voice, indeed, is what seems most absent. In Johnson's diction and form, vernacular is almost entirely submerged in memorial precision; dialectical invention and altiloquence give way to concertized voicing and diction as he invents a cultivated equivalent to the classic African-American sermon that ran from the Creation to Judgment Day in an electrifying pastiche.

Consider, for example, the following lines from Johnson's poem "The Crucifixion":

> And the veil of the temple was split in two,
> The midday sun refused to shine,
> The thunder rumbled and the lightning wrote
> An unknown language in the sky.
> What a day! Lord, what a day!
> When my blessed Jesus died.
>
> Oh, I tremble, yes, I tremble,
> It causes me to tremble, tremble,
> When I think how Jesus died;
> Died on the steeps of Calvary,
> How Jesus died for sinners,
> Sinners like you and me.

Now, Hurston's (or Lovelace's) version of the same scene:

> And about dat time
> De angel of Justice unsheathed his flamin' sword and
>   ripped de veil of de temple
> And de High Priest vacated his office
> And then de sacrificial energy penetrated de mighty strata

And quickened de bones of de prophets
And they arose from their graves and walked about in de
   streets of Jerusalem
I heard de whistle of de damnation train
Dat pulled out from [de] Garden of Eden loaded wid cargo
   goin' to hell
Ran at break-neck speed all de way thru de law
All de way thru de prophetic age
All de way thru de reign of kings and judges—
Plowed her way thru de Jurdan
And on her way to Calvary, when she blew for de switch
Jesus stood out on her track like a rough-backed mountain
And she threw her cow-catcher in His side and His blood
   ditched de train
He died for our sins.

The extraordinary extended figure of the damnation train, to be discussed later for its relevance to other parts of *Jonah's Gourd Vine*, is characteristic of the language Hurston employs in her complex embellishment of the Crucifixion. But even in small tropes—"sacrificial energy" penetrating the "mighty strata" rather than "lightning" writing an "unknown language" in the sky, for example—Hurston's passage calls for contemplation of its far more complicated allegorical layers. This is not Johnson's best passage, but neither is it Hurston's; yet both are representative. To the extent that we are justified in ascribing the language to Hurston, rather than to C. C. Lovelace, the passage no doubt signifies upon Johnson's pallid dramatization, which one might say, to paraphrase Hurston, only "passes for colored."

More to the point, however, is the fact that Hurston's orthography, her variations in person and tense, and her lack of grammatical markers or punctuating line stops—that is, her unmistakable but also flexible appeal to dialect—support the vividly inventive metaphors of her scene. Here and elsewhere, her use of enjambment, repetition, assonance, and a metrical scheme based on breathing rather than syllabic count drive the verse into a form that is "readable" only to the degree that it is "heard." The African-American sermon, as she wrote in "The Sanctified Church," an essay unpublished in her lifetime, is "drama with music." The vernacular of the Lovelace sermon, far from suggesting the pathos or humor that Johnson feared it was always in danger of provoking, more exactly realizes the power Johnson himself attributed to the folk preachers when he said: "They were all saturated with the sublime phraseology of the Hebrew prophets and steeped in the idioms of King James English, so when they preached and warmed to their work they spoke another language, a language far removed from traditional Negro dialect." The point here, of course, is not to dismiss Johnson's fine volume or the rationale for his choice to eschew dialect but rather to indicate the manner in which Hurston intuitively grasped the limitations of Johnson's theory and returned directly to the vocal powers of vernacular culture for her inspiration in *Jonah's Gourd Vine* and elsewhere, making herself, as Du Bois might have said, "bone of the bone and flesh of the flesh of them that live within the Veil." Before returning to look in more detail at the Lovelace sermon and its role in Hurston's composition of *Jonah's Gourd Vine*, several other crucial Africanist elements of her theory adumbrated in the novel must be considered.

•   •   •

When the congregation at Notasulga discovers that young John Pearson has a "good strainin' voice," they call on him more frequently to offer prayer, and John responds with some "new figure, some new praise-giving name for God" each time he kneels.

Hurston writes: "He rolled his African drum up to the altar, and called his Congo Gods by Christian names. One night at the altar-call he cried out his barbaric poetry to his 'Wonder-workin' God so effectively that three converts came thru [to] religion under the sound of his voice." The quality of John's voice becomes Hurston's main focus, but her characterization of it as an African drum and her deliberate fusion of African and Puritan traditions constitute a miniature historical essay on the role of religion in slave acculturation. Likewise, the "barbaric poetry" of his idiom is a virtual quotation from numerous ethnographic essays on black language at the turn of the century. There is no indication that this is conscious on John's part; indeed, the fact that it is unconscious may be crucial, for Hurston was concerned to register African retentions as a powerful, formative undercurrent or syncretism that had been thoroughly absorbed in Afro-Christian practice. Her introduction of a theory of retentions, however, was peculiarly conscious, even forced, according to those readers who have been at a loss to explain Hurston's blunt ethnographic intrusions into her narrative. Yet abrupt though it is, the characterization of John's voice as an African drum goes to the very heart of the leadership and sermonic power that he comes to epitomize.

The more dramatic figuration of the African drum appears in the context of the feast held after the cotton is in. Spurning fiddles, guitars, and banjoes—"us ain't no white folks," they say—the people clap and dance:

> They called for the instrument that they had brought to America in their skins—the drum—and they played upon it. With their hands they played upon the little dance drums of Africa. The drums of kid-skin. With their feet they stomped it, and the voice of Kata-Kumba, the great drum, lifted itself within them and they heard it. The great drum that is made by priests and sits in

majesty in the juju house. The drum with the man skin that is dressed with human blood, that is beaten with a human shin-bone and speaks to gods as a man and to men as a God. Then they beat upon the drum and danced. It was said, "He will serve us better if we bring him from Africa nameless and thing-less." So the buckra reasoned. They tore away his clothes that Cuffy might bring nothing away, but Cuffy seized his drum and hid it in his skin under the skull bones. The shin-bones he bore openly, for he thought, "Who shall rob me of shin-bones when they see no drum?" So he laughed with cunning and said, "I, who am borne away to become an orphan, carry my parents with me. For Rhythm is she not my mother and Drama is [he not] her man?" So he groaned aloud in the ships and hid his drum and laughed.

Appearing virtually out of nowhere in the text, this passage is sometimes cited as evidence of Hurston's as yet immature skill at integrating ethnological observation into fictional narrative. Indeed, the passage introduces a flurry of authorial observations about the African roots of black folksinging and dancing, interspersed among the recorded stanzas and ornamented dialogue, and written in what appears to be a kind of fieldwork shorthand: "Hollow-hand clapping for the bass notes. Heel and toe stomping for the little ones. Ibo tune corrupted with Nango. Congo gods talking in Alabama. . . . Too hot for words. Fiery drum clapping." Hurston is frequently an "observer" in the novel, however, and *Jonah's Gourd Vine* a palimpsest of autobiographical and cultural rumination that not only fuses her family history to fieldwork and theory but, in fact, self-consciously extends the attack on the boundary between ethnology and narrative that she had begun in *Mules and Men* (1935), which was written before but published after *Jonah's Gourd Vine*.

Supported by other minor allusions to the rhythm and tonality of drumbeats in the novel, these passages about African drumming are a pointed assertion of African retentions at a moment when the issue continued to be hotly debated. The writers of the Harlem Renaissance, typified by Alain Locke's classic anthology *The New Negro* (1925), frequently argued for the African roots of black art and music; Du Bois had offered clear points of departure in *The Souls of Black Folk* and then again more emphatically in *The Negro* (1915); and Carter Woodson, Melville Herskovits, and others would soon provide invaluable studies of African retentions. At the same time, the dominant view, certainly among most white sociologists and cultural critics, was that African Americans had been divested of their ancestral culture by the ordeal of slavery. The influential sociologist Robert E. Park claimed, for example, that African Americans were entirely estranged from their ancestral land, languages, and cultural traditions; and the eminent historian U. B. Phillips claimed that African Americans were "as completely broken from their tribal stems as if they had been brought from the planet Mars." I am less concerned here with the lines of this debate, however, than with Hurston's deployment of retentions as a particular weapon against the calculated destruction of culture that accompanied slavery. Stripped of the apparent "clothes" of culture, rendered "thing-less," as Hurston's drum passage held, Africans nonetheless carried with them vital traditions figured as the "parents" of Rhythm and Drama, which are central elements of black folk culture as it is analyzed in her essays and in the performance of John Pearson in *Jonah's Gourd Vine*. Although Hurston's fieldwork as it was recorded in *Mules and Men* and especially in her Caribbean volume, *Tell My Horse* (1938), charts linguistic and material survivals with some precision, the passages in the novel, like the essays in Cunard's *Negro*, amount to finely condensed philosophical statements.

What is most notable about Hurston's theory of survivals is that it often dwells especially in the world of the phenomenal rather than the concrete. In her 1943 essay "High John de Conquer," named for the legendary root of black conjure and luck, her personification of High John as a mythic figure accompanying Africans on the middle passage endows him, like the trickster figures of the animal tales, with sacred properties, making him an incarnation of the voice that "has evaded the ears of white people" and borne up black people. The spiritual sustenance and secret powers that he provides his folk—including the signifying power of black laughter and black song—in the new world of enslavement Hurston can trace only to a primordial world of occluded memory, originating existence. Before he is reborn a "natural" man and a trickster who can always get past Old Massa, High John is "a whisper, a will to hope, a wish to find something worthy of laughter and song. Then the whisper put on flesh. His footsteps sounded across the world in a low but musical rhythm as if the world he walked on was a singing-drum." Alongside the "black bodies huddled down there [in the ships' holds] in the middle passage, being hauled across the water to helplessness," High John came "walking on the waves of sound . . . walking the very winds that filled the sails of the ships." The fascinating High John essay, only touched on here, rewrites the drum passage of *Jonah's Gourd Vine* into an allegory of retentions (and physical survival), and it does so by locating the origin of African-American songmaking and storytelling, especially trickster tales and Master-John stories, in *spirit* itself: the wind and the waves of sound that carry High John across the Atlantic yoke the breath of the body, the whisper of life, and the singing sound of African drums. High John, in this configuration, *is* spirit or soul, the rhythm of black life in the voice that links body to drum, mediating between humans and gods, as between language and sound.

The High John essay clarifies Hurston's intentions in *Jonah's Gourd Vine* by demonstrating just how the Lovelace sermon and John Pearson's straining voice are to be read as marked by significant African retentions. Interchangeable figures for one another, drum and body form a single communicative medium that carries African spirit in a New World form, the voice internalizing the rhythm of drumming. The trope of African drums appearing in the work of both black and white writers such as Langston Hughes, Arna Bontemps, Eugene O'Neill, and Vachel Lindsay had nearly been drained of significance by the vogue of primitivism in the 1920s, and one can be certain that Hurston intended to redress the easily misconstrued use of drumming and thereby reanimate the observation of William Arms Fisher in his 1926 collection, *Seventy Negro Spirituals*: "The unseen ghost of the crude African drum walks in the midst of all [the Negro's] poetry and music." Crude of course it was not; but Hurston's contribution was to fuse an awareness of the rhythm and tonality of African drumming in slave culture, where drums were frequently prohibited, to those strategies of subversion, indirection, and secrecy retained in later vernacular culture.

Hurston's drum passage, less so her High John de Conquer allegory, takes for granted the communicative power of drumming— the capacity of African drums to "talk" in a coded language of rhythm and timbre. Although Henry Krehbiel among others had already made tentative associations between the vocalism of African drum language and African-American cultural forms, the considerable debate about the role of African polyrhythms and blue tonality in black American music, and hence the links between drum and voice in the formation of jazz, was not far advanced when Hurston wrote. As in the case of Du Bois, however, her interest in the roots of black music was less musicological than epistemological. That is to say, she wanted to suggest that black folk vernacular was informed, whether with full consciousness or not, by a spirit that broke down boundaries—at extremity the boundaries of consciousness, opening in worship or performance into the ecstasy of possession. The folk spirit, moreover, was closer to ancestral memories, as Hurston contended in "The Sanctified Church" (an essay that in turn borrowed from *Jonah's Gourd Vine*), where she wrote that "the Negro has not been christianized as extensively as is generally believed. The great masses are still standing before their pagan altars and calling old gods by a new name. As evidence of this, note the drum-like rhythm of all Negro spirituals." The phrase "the drum with the man skin" therefore refers at once to an ancestral drum, held in its sacred precinct and used ceremonially, and to the African-American body in New World slave culture. Although the context of Afro-Caribbean religious practice makes for a symbology distinct from that of the American South, Hurston put it more forthrightly in her later description of a Jamaican dance in *Tell My Horse*: "The drums and the movements of the dancers draw so close together that the drums become people and the people become drums. The pulse of the drum is their shoulders and belly. Truly the drum is inside their bodies." The sign of internalized inheritances that are at once intensely spiritual and practical—with drums lost or prohibited by the slaveholding regime, percussion depended on different instruments: tools, household utensils, hands, and feet—the body as drum becomes the primary site of cultural production, a reservoir of the ancestral and an instrument of re-creation.

The fact that song and drumming together entered so fully into African-American life can be traced to the centrality of music in black labor, beginning in Africa and transformed under slavery. In *Jonah's Gourd Vine* this stands forth in several signal instances, most of all in John's brief experience working on the railroad gang at Sanford. For Hurston, as for other African-American writers, the railroad and train are powerful symbols—powerful in *Jonah's Gourd Vine* to the point of being baroque but not, as some have argued, awkward. Hurston makes the trope of the railroad first of all the crucible of African-American vernacular song—a crossroads of "locomotive energies," as Houston Baker has written in his more general theory of a blues vernacular. The work of lining track makes for a long day of "strain, sweat and rhythm," the men grunting over the lining bar and swinging the nine-pound hammer to drive spike after spike: "Another rail spiked down. Another offering to the soul of civilization whose other name is travel," as Hurston codified the rhythmic labor of the road gang in *Dust Tracks on the Road*. Hurston's repetition of the word "straining," as well as her focus on the hammer's swing and the overt musical punning in her description of the communal labor—"then a rhythmic shaking of the nine-hundred-pound rail by bearing down on the bars thrust under it in concert"—alert us to the cognate rhythmic labor, straining, and bearing up that will appear in the preacher's sermonic performance, which, like the spirituals, has embedded in it the percussive reminders of ancestral drumming.

The railroad camp, in fact, provides John Pearson a springboard to the pulpit. After hearing the Sanford minister one Sunday, John returns to camp and repreaches the sermon himself, perfectly "marking" the minister; soon he announces his call to preach, is ordained, and moves into his leadership role. The point of this episode, however, is not just to get John Pearson into the pulpit, but to demonstrate the origins—or at least the primary analogues— of his vocal arts in black labor itself. Hurston no doubt drew on the title poem of Sterling Brown's volume *Southern Road* (1932), with its striking connection of work-song rhythm and diction to versified form:

Swing dat hammer—hunh—
Steady, bo';
Swing dat hammer—hunh—
Steady, bo';
Ain't no rush, bebby,
Long ways to go. . . .

The rhythmic iteration of the hammer strike accompanied by the grunting expulsion of breath reappears in Hurston's comparable description of the gang hammering and "singing" the rail into place in a kind of kinaesthetic blues:

"Oh, Lulu!"
"Hanh!" A spike gone under John's sledge.
"Oh, oh, gal!"
"Hanh!"
"Want to see you!"
"Hanh!"
"So bad!"
"Hanh!"

Although some of the spirituals derived from or overlapped with work songs—"Michael Row Your Boat Ashore," for instance— James Weldon Johnson distinguished the swing common to each form, and his account of the fusion of labor and aesthetic form in the road gang is particularly insightful:

All the men sing and move together as they swing their picks or rock-breaking hammers. They move like a ballet; not a ballet of cavorting legs and pirouetting feet, but a ballet of bending backs and quivering muscles. It is all in rhythm but a rhythm impossible to set down. There is always a leader and he sets the pace. A phrase is sung while the shining hammers are being lifted. It is cut off suddenly as the hammers begin to descend and gives place to a prolonged grunt which becomes explosive at the impact of the blow. Each phrase of the song is independent, apparently obeying no law of time. After each impact the hammers lie still and there is silence. As they begin to rise again the next phrase of the song is sung; and so on. . . . There are variations that violate the obvious laws of rhythm, but over it all can be discerned a superior rhythmic law.

Such an overarching but unidentifiable law of rhythm, which was to become a central feature of jazz theory, was frequently attributed to the "authentic" spirituals. In his contemporary account of the Fisk Jubilee Singers, *The Story of the Jubilee Singers and Their Songs* (1881), for example, J. B. T. Marsh spoke of the "higher law of rhythmic flow," the broken and irregular but nonetheless exact swaying time, that governed the spirituals. Johnson's analysis is most pertinent because it points both to the instrumentality of the body in labor—its equivalence to tools—and to the regulation of each by song. The hidden rhythmic law is marked by the punctuations of breath: the straining of the road gang is recapitulated in the straining of the preacher when he enters fully upon the labor of his sermon, and the "hanh" of the railroad song becomes the "ha" of the Lovelace sermon, as Hurston first transcribed it and then gave it to John Pearson.

In Dogon belief of West Africa, the hammer of the blacksmith creates primal energy; his anvil was the first drum, and the re-creation of the blows of the sacred hammer reminds men of the spiritual beginnings of the world, just as the drums in certain instances are used to summon the ancestors. Other lines might be drawn between hammering, drumming, and oratory—the Bambara, for instance, call the griot the "blacksmith of the word"—but no particular African mythology need be located in order to sense the network of associations bound to John Pearson, the "drum with the man skin," who also speaks "to gods as a man and to men as a God." Hurston's mind, in fact, is fixed as much on the attenuation as on the repetition of Africanisms in black American culture. Noting the great proliferation of railroad themes and railroad sounds in blues and jazz, Albert Murray has argued that "what may once have been West African drum talk" has "long since become the locomotive talk . . . heard by down-home blackfolk on farms, in work camps, and on the outskirts of southern towns." Hurston seems to have apprehended something quite similar in her depiction of the onomatopoeic "chanting" of the train, as she calls it, with which John Pearson is continually fascinated: "Soon in the distance he heard the whistle, 'Wah-ooom! Wahup, wahup!' And around the bend came first the smoke stack, belching smoke and flames of fire. The drivers turning over chanting 'Opelika-black-and-dirty! Opelika-black-and-dirty.' Then as she pulled into the station, the powerful whisper of steam. Start-ing off again, 'Wolf coming! Wolf coming! Wolf coming! Opelika-black-and-dirty, Opelika-black-and-dirty! Auh—wah-hoooon'—into the great away that gave John's feet such a yearning for distance." Likewise, the primordial energy of hammer and drum have long since moved into John Pearson's voice, where the ser-monic form, with its own incorporation of the rhythms of the work song, carried from the middle passage through slavery and beyond, transfigures the intricate dexterity of song into verbal per-formance, as the preacher speaks, chants, and sings the story of creation, deliverance, and judgment:

> Jesus have always loved us from the foundation of the world
> When God
> Stood out on the apex of His power
> Before the hammers of creation
> Fell upon the anvils of Time and hammered out the ribs
>   of the earth . . .

•   •   •

John Pearson's delivery of the Lovelace sermon caps his oratorical rehabilitation of his career. His extraordinary abilities with speech and his fulfilling a function in the community that is both sacramental and performative override his moral failings, his indulgence in the sexual pleasures of a "natchel man." "When Ah speak tuh yuh from dis pulpit," he reminds the congregation earlier, "dat ain't me talkin', dat's de voice uh God speakin' thru me." His sermons mimic God's voice, and if no one believes in such literal prophetism, it is nonetheless true that John Pearson is the bard of his people, his ability to "talk" encompassing the biblical history of enslavement and delivery in the voice of the black ancestors. Hurston's novelistic delivery of the Lovelace sermon adds to this a conscious framing of John's role and a conscious appropriation of its power to her own narrative art, as well as a critique of her capacity to represent the sermonic performance in literary form.

Despite his bardic cultural function, John's redemptive role is robbed of its mythic significance by the narrative life in which his sermon is inscribed. The elaborate trope of the "damnation train," whose cowcatcher pierces Jesus' side and releases his sacrificial blood in the Lovelace sermon, is reduced to a burlesque figure in the train that smashes into John's Cadillac after his last act of infidelity. The long-standing resonance of the train as a figure of black deliverance in the spirituals ("Same Train," "Get on Board, Little Chillen," and so on), its rich association with movement and migration in modern black history, its embodiment in work songs and the blues of the endless toil of black America—all these associations, which Hurston calls into view over the course of the novel before concentrating their energy into the judgment train of the sermon, are diminished in the comic instrument of reprisal. Hurston thus looked askance at her father, whose moral character is judged harshly in *Jonah's Gourd Vine*, but also at the privileged power accorded the male preacher in the African-American tradition as she had experienced it. By signifying upon that power, however, she also paid tribute to it, joining the preacher's voice provisionally to her own in order to measure the differences between them, to interrogate and preserve the formative power of Afro-Christianity incarnate in the sermonic utterance she sought to rival.

Hurston's interest in the sermon as a vernacular form, then, lay not simply in her sense that it was brilliant verbal art but also in her belief that it contained echoes of African ancestry that were dim but still fundamental and that it offered a continual recomposition of the structuring mythology of black America in which she could participate as a writer and as a woman. The "hammers of creation" in the Lovelace sermon merge an African retention quite explicitly with the work songs of the road gang and a unique mythologizing of the Christian creation. In addition, the "hammers" tie John Pearson, through the medium of his intoning voice, to God's own creativity, a fact further supported by the striking plural—"Jesus have always loved us"—which refers not just to Father and Son or the Trinity but also to John, whose self-serving "wounds of Jesus" sermon is meant to regain the good will of his congregation, who will forgive his marital infidelities—who will even, for that matter, participate in them as they make him the heroic spokesman of their sacred story. Above all, Hurston's adducement of the African source of John's sermonic talent, the most pronounced revision she makes in transferring the Lovelace sermon from the Cunard anthology to *Jonah's Gourd Vine*, is a way to deepen and strengthen the legitimacy and independence of African-American language as an ancestral inheritance capable of transcending slavery and Jim Crow.

If Hurston's novel offers one of the first lengthy dramatizations of black vernacular free from the garbled stereotypes of minstrelsy and plantation mythology, foregrounding black talk among characters and subsuming that same talk into its narrative voice, it also takes its lead from the critical role played by the voice of the preacher throughout the history of African Americans. First analyzed in detail by Du Bois and brought to the fore later in the twentieth century by the national prominence in the Civil Rights movement of Martin Luther King, Jr., and other ministers in the Southern Christian Leadership Conference, the preacher's status as community spokesman was hardly uncomplicated in cultural representations when Hurston came to it. Minstrelsy and nineteenth-century plantation revues such as A. G. Field's "Darkest America" often included burlesque black sermons, full of comically twisted theology and pathetic malapropisms. For many white Americans, such caricatures endorsed Puckett's view that Negro speech was a "labyrinth of jaw-breaking words full of sound and fury." (Even well-intentioned white replications of the black sermon went awry. For example, Vachel Lindsay's "How Samson Bore Away the Gates of Gaza," subtitled "a Negro sermon" and appearing in *Poetry* in 1917, styled Samson a "bold Jack-Johnson Israelite," but Lindsay lamented his inability to capture the language; and Natalie Curtis responded in *Poetry* two months later with an actual black spiritual version of Samson as a Negro, including a legitimate rendition of "Ride On, Jesus," which Lindsay had alluded to in his poem.) In addition, black folklore in the early twentieth century increasingly included tales of preacher humor, primarily devoted to corruption and sexual escapades, indicating a decline in faith and a fragmentation of the Afro-Christian basis of the black community. At the same time, however, the *Southern Workman* and other journals had begun by the turn of the century to feature essays on African-American preachers and preaching, recognizing it as a grand vernacular art as much deserving of preservation and study as the spirituals. The nineteenth-century Virginia preacher John Jasper, whose famous sermon "De Sun Do Move an' De Earth Am Square" had been published as early as

1882 and which Johnson described in his preface to *God's Trombones*, was the subject of a biographical and rhetorical study that transcribed a group of his sermons in 1908. Perhaps most important of all in spurring Hurston's decision to feature the sermon, however, was the advent of recorded African-American sermons. The some 750 sermons recorded between 1926 and 1938 were part of the greater vogue among the black population, North and South alike, of "race records"—blues, spirituals (or gospel), folk-singing, and sermons directed primarily to a black listening audience on major and minor labels beginning with Okeh in 1923. (The Black Swan company, the single black-owned label, advertised itself as "The Only Genuine Colored Record. Others Are Only Passing for Colored.") Among the many other sermonic themes recorded in the 1920s, one might note especially the Reverend J. M. Gates's hugely popular "Death's Black Train Is Coming," as well as the Reverend A. W. Nix's "The Black Diamond Express to Hell" and its counterpart "The White Flyer to Heaven." Just this dualism of the damnation train and the salvation train, a staple in the sermonic tradition, appears in one of Lovelace's most complex images, near the conclusion of his sermon:

> When we shall all be delegates, ha!
> To dat Judgment Convention
> When de two trains of Time shall meet on de trestle
> And wreck de burning axles of de unformed ether
> And de mountains shall skip like lambs . . .

Any complete account of the significance of Hurston's reproduction of the Lovelace sermon in her first novel would thus have to place it in relation to the widespread and complex role that sermons have played in defining the creative limits of African-American expression in many other artistic genres, all of which have drawn power from the preacher's performative eloquence.

The inclusion of African-American sermons on race records is particularly important because sound recording itself had a dual role that facilitated both the collection of folklore and its commercial dissemination. Hurston herself reported to her mentor, Franz Boas, on the prevalence of phonographs among the southern black population; and although her own fieldwork at that point relied on memorization and notebooks (in 1935 she would assist Alan Lomax in recording sermons and songs in Florida), the competition between printed and aural forms of transmission surely entered into her aesthetic as well. Following her own rule, Hurston herself might have designated the Lovelace sermon a "neo-sermon," for the printed sermon stands in much the same relation to its actual performance as did the published "neo-spirituals" to the authentic songs of the folk. The popular Fisk and Hampton collections of spirituals, Jeanette Robinson Murphy noted laconically in a seminal 1899 article, provided no instructions as to the irregular phrasing, "undulations," and "trimmings" common to black singing; nor did they advise the uninitiated how to "sing tones not found in our [European] scale," or indicate that "by some mysterious power, to be learned only from the negro," the singer "should carry over his breath from line to line and from verse to verse, even at the risk of bursting a blood-vessel," at length giving way to "peculiar humming sound—'hum-m-m-m.'" (Murphy's tongue-in-cheek analysis did not undercut her profound admiration for the true style of the spirituals, and her essay was among the first to make a serious case for African retentions in song and folklore.) Likewise, the key for Hurston or other transcribers of sermons was to capture the performative aspects of the sermon and, while avoiding the pitfalls of dialect, to reproduce on the page the vocal characteristics of the sermon that locate it midway between song and speech, as declamation gives way to recitative and "intoning"—those elusive "intonations and delicate variations" that William Allen, as early as 1867 in *Slave Songs in the United States*, had said "cannot be reproduced on paper."

Studies of the African-American sermon have traced its intoning form to African chants of tribal law and communal praise poems; detected in its harmonics the blues tetrachord of the work songs, field hollers, and some spirituals; and associated its tonal improvisations with the beginnings of vocal and instrumental jazz. One may sense all these possibilities in the Lovelace-Pearson sermon, where God's labor from the beginning of time, and Christ's suffering redemption, also present from the beginning of time, are combined into a drama of communal delivery in which the preacher essentially reenacts the entire biblical saga. He does so in order to reenforce the long-standing analogy between the delivery from pharaonic bondage and the African-American delivery from slavery; but it is the originality of the story, its improvisation and exposed architectonics, that most fuel the performance. The sermon, that is to say, embellishes both the creation and the Bible, the preacher's labor uniting the hammer and anvil, the drum and shinbone, reinventing the white man's central mythology in each telling. The sign of that labor, as in the structure of the work song, is the preacher's "straining," the irregular but rhythmic inhalations and exhalations marked on the page by "ah!" and "ha!":

> Who shall I make him after? Ha!
> Worlds within worlds began to wheel and roll
> De Sun, Ah!
> Gethered up de fiery skirts of her garments
> And wheeled around de throne, Ah!
> Saying, Ah, make man after me, ha!
> God gazed upon the sun
> And sent her back to her blood-red socket
> And shook His head, ha! . . .

"Negro singing and formal speech are breathy," Hurston writes in "Spirituals and Neo-Spirituals." "The audible breathing is part of the performance and various devices are resorted to to adorn the breath taking." At length, the embellishment of breathing gives way to a humming or moaning that, in Hurston's apt metaphor, "liquifies" words into a pure vocal music, whose timbre might be traced to the nontempered scale of African music but whose erasure of traditional linguistic structures and sounds is specifically African American. Hurston's own annotation on "straining," in the glossary of *Jonah's Gourd Vine*, is relevant here: "In his cooler passages the colored preacher attempts to achieve what to him is grammatical correctness, but as he warms up he goes natural. The 'ha' in the sermon marks a breath. The congregation likes to hear the preacher breathing or straining."

Hurston's characterization at once underscores the performative aspect of the sermon—in its relation to a sort of folk theater and in the audience's choral role—and makes evident the link between sheer tonalities and the altiloquence, the highly figurative, sometimes neological expressions that mark the sermon. Such invention in diction and syntax, as in the acceleration into chant or song, amounts to "recomposing America in terms of Africa," to borrow an idea from Ben Sidran's *Black Talk*. One can see this in a number of phrases, lines, and passages from the sermon that depend on figurative leaps—semantic as well as rhythmic enjambments that reconfigure Protestant mythology, suffusing Bible language with the inventions of the black spirituals and a willful adornment of the text in a speakerly voice, as in the passage following Jesus' appeal to God, "Why hast thou forsaken me?":

> The mountains fell to their rocky knees and trembled like a
>   beast
> From the stroke of the master's axe
> One angel took the flinches of God's eternal power
> And bled the veins of the earth
> One angel that stood at the gate with a flaming sword
> Was so well pleased with his power

Until he pierced the moon with his sword
And she ran down in blood
And de sun
Batted her fiery eyes and put on her judgement robe
And laid down in de cradle of eternity
And rocked herself into sleep and slumber
He died until the great belt in the wheel of time
And de geological strata fell aloose . . .
And de orchestra had struck silence for the space of half an
hour
Angels had lifted their harps to de weepin' willows . . .

Among other remarkable reconfigurations in this passage dramatizing Christ's Passion, Lovelace, or Hurston, unites the gospels
with apposite prophetic and apocalyptic scripture (Joel 2:30–31,
Acts 2:20, and Revelation 6:12); borrows elements from both the
powerful imagery of Protestant hymnology and such black spirituals as "My Lord, What a Morning" or "Stars in the Elements"
("The stars in the elements are falling / And the moon drips away
into blood"), "See How They Done My Lord" ("They pierced him
in the side, / an' He never said a mumbalin' word / The blood
came twinklin' down"), " 'Zekiel Saw the Wheel" (" 'Zekiel saw de
wheel of time"), and "O Rocks Don't Fall On Me" ("O, in dat great
great judgment day / Rocks and mountains don't fall on me"); and
personifies a millennial time associated in Afro-Christian thought
with redemption from slavery and its long aftermath.

In this passage as in others, however, the sermon's precise
sources are purposefully obscured by the syntactical slippage
and fusion of idea with incantatory sound, a strategy with African
roots but specifically African-American significance. The Lovelace sermon is an excellent example of the black preacher's creative recomposition of the Bible's narrative, frequently a complex
and elusive performance that, as Hortense Spillers has argued,

represents his ambivalent apprenticeship to, and thus his herme-neutical play with, the central mythos of white culture. The closer the preacher moves to the tonal semantics of singing, the more fully he embodies ancestral arts and Africanizes American experi-ence. In Africa the communal and historical storyteller, the griot, displays an exemplary command of circumlocution and oratori-cal wit that are taken to be extensions of the primal energy of sound itself, the force of *nommo* harnassed to the medium of communal memory. The form and structure of such talent sur-vive in some instances of the black sermon, put in the service of reimagining America's founding theological mythos. "While he lives and moves in the midst of a white civilization," Hurston re-marked in "Characteristics of Negro Expression," everything that [the Negro] touches is re-interpreted for his own use." From this perspective, the movement into a metadiction or into vocalization is a means to reach back toward ancestral tonality, to recite the Christian story in terms of black bondage, and to signify upon the constricting bonds of the master's cultural language.

· · ·

"Mimicry is an art in itself," Hurston contended in the same essay. Her notion has a range of implications that could include refer-ence to the appearance of African retentions in African-American art; to black dialect as a creative mimicry of white English, as well as the disputed and now generally disavowed belief that the black spirituals and folktales were simply recastings of Euro-American materials; and, in the case of the sermon, to a parallel impro-visation upon the text of scripture. Mimicry as Hurston defines it could also encompass her contention that, like the preacher's taking of his text, certain "visions" accompanying conversion in black religion had become virtually formulaic. "I knew them by heart as did the rest of the congregation," she recalled of the visions attested to in her father's church. "Some [converts] would forget a part and improvise clumsily or fill up the gap with shouting. The audience knew, but everybody acted as if every word of it was new." Too, mimicry was integral to the folk arts Hurston recorded: the trickster and Master-John tales of *Mules and Men*, which thrived on signifying combat with the white man, were built by the cyclic tale telling of the "lying" sessions that were the foundation of Hurston's collecting and her own writing. All these elements of mimicry bear on the composition of *Jonah's Gourd Vine* and Hurston's insertion into the novel of the Lovelace sermon, elevating the novel, like the sermon, into the grandest "lying" and further eroding the distinction between fiction and folklore. Indeed, the force of mimicry, in both its aesthetic and ideological contours, appears nowhere more emphatically than in the very fact of Hurston's professional status, straddling the borderline between anthropology and literature.

In both "Spirituals and Neo-Spirituals" and her later essay "The Sanctified Church," Hurston was quick to satirize white singing, prayer, and preaching as dull and predictable, lacking in spontaneity and imagination: A white sermon, she derisively said, was more likely to be a "lecture," just the sort of flat ethnological exhibit she hoped to avoid in her own writing. Notably, that is what the congregation charges against John Pearson's competitor, the Reverend Cozy, who is brought in to unseat John—to cut down "dis Jonah's gourd vine," as they interpret the scripture—after many in the community blame John for Lucy's death, condemning his infidelity and his quick marriage to Hattie. Cozy mistakes his audience, but more than that, Hurston suggests, he mistakes his calling when he competes against John. "Ahm a race man! Ah solves the race problem," Cozy exclaims, and his sermon proceeds to indulge in revisionist statements about black history and black theology. A full five minutes into Cozy's nationalist sermon, one sister whispers to another, "Ah ain't heard whut de tex' wuz." Hurston's own cynicism about Race Men no doubt enters into her portrait of Cozy. "The Race Leader is a fiction that is good only at the political trough," she would write in *Dust Tracks on the Road*, and she had already satirized Marcus Garvey in the late 1920s. But more to the point, Cozy's "lecture" lacks the very essence of the sermonic performance. Because his "handlin' de Alphabets" does not spring from scripture, he fails his audience, who demand the formulaic act of the minister heard by John early in his apprenticeship: "Ah takes mah tex' and Ah takes mah time. . . . Ah takes mah tex' 'tween de lids of de Bible. . . . Long ez Ah gives yuh de word uh Gawd, 'tain't none uh yo' business whar Ah gits it from." John Pearson is able to destroy Cozy with a mere rendition of "Dry Bones," his own best sermon but also a highly conventionalized one in the sermonic literature.

The preacher's ritualized act of "taking his text" provides a starting point for his performance—a highly structured moment giving way to a flowing, undulating song-story that, like a controlled improvisation, follows expected chord changes and an identifiable melody but rearranges both. Hurston, it may be said, does much the same thing with the Lovelace sermon, though the question arises: is it Lovelace or Hurston whose sermon we read? and what does her act of appropriation, her mimicry, signify? Hurston's role in the sermon has to be pronounced. Although she drew it more or less directly from her field notes, according to Robert Hemenway, it is Hurston who set the sermon in verse, marking Lovelace's straining, choosing orthographic signals of his dialect, and, quite possibly, modifying his altiloquent diction. The Lovelace sermon, in the Cunard anthology, is pointedly labeled "as heard by Zora Neale Hurston," which, as Robert Stepto has noted, should alert us both to the homage paid to Lovelace's voice and to the likelihood that the sermon was not exactly "recorded" but probably rephrased by its skilled, inventive listener. (In addition, although the sermon is not short compared with those issued on race records, neither is it long by sermonic standards—or by the later recorded standard, for example, of the popular contemporary black preacher C. L. Franklin—and it is therefore probable that Hurston condensed as well as rephrased Lovelace's words.) The transition from prose to verse is at once the moment Lovelace goes "natural," as Hurston puts it, and the moment she herself enters into the creation of the sermon, joining her own authorial voice to his. In that conjunction lies a series of complicated mimetic negotiations that epitomize Hurston's part in the creation and sustenance of African-American cultural expression.

One of Hurston's first articles, an interview with Cudjo Lewis, the only remaining survivor of the last ship to carry African slaves directly to the United States in 1859, was substantially plagiarized from a published book of sketches about the old South. One could suggest that what Hurston discovered in the course of writing *Mules and Men* was how to plagiarize professionally and ethically, so to speak, by utilizing what she called the "spyglass of Anthropology." What is remarkable about *Mules and Men*, however, is the degree of Hurston's personal immersion in the culture she studies; the effectiveness of her collecting lay in her willingness and ability to enter the folk culture of the South, to rely on her own verbal skills and on memory for her record, and finally to participate personally in the tale-telling art she was collecting, to the point of rewriting the context and even the language in which tales were told to give them more clarity and drama. Hurston was clearly capable of careful, painstaking ethnology. Her essays "Conversion" and "Shouting" in the Cunard anthology, for example, resemble case studies to the point of near parody. But it was the liminal terrain between the analytic and the poetic that most engaged Hurston's sympathies, as it was the act of translating from the oral to the written, from black folk culture to the largely white commercial and professional world of her career, that most deserves our attention as an act of mimicry. Just as Lovelace (or John Pearson) "takes his text" from scripture before setting off on an improvised flight that molds the Bible to his own inventive use, Hurston "takes her text" from the folkloric record before gathering it into the compass of her personal narrative in *Mules and Men*, or appropriating it to the voice of a fictional character in *Jonah's Gourd Vine*, or in the grandest such gesture of incorporation rewriting the biblical delivery of the Israelites as allegorical black history in *Moses, Man of the Mountain* (1939). Cheryl Wall has convincingly argued that Hurston's use of the "Behold de Rib!" sermon in *Mules and Men*—a sermon that makes woman the equal of man ("God Amighty, he took de bone out of [Adam's] side / So dat places de woman beside us")—represents her own acquisition of a professional storytelling voice. Just so, Hurston's mimicry—her recapitulation of black folklore in the modulation of printed form—stands on the razor-thin line between revelation and preservation, performance and concealment, extending the "lying" of the folk into the domain of white commerce, which, as both her notoriously manipulative patronage by Mrs. Osgood Mason and even her mentoring by Boas taught her, had the ring of neoslavery. In both *Mules and Men* and *Jonah's Gourd Vine*, Hurston provides a glossary of terms and intrudes authorially to explain dialect expressions; but because she does not do so methodically or consistently, such ethnological devices, like her adoption of dialectical figures in her narrative voice, tend to reinforce as much as to lessen the uninformed reader's exclusion from the transcribed world of vernacular. In speaking the dialect of folk culture, she elevated it above ethnological curiosity even as she limited its inherent mutability and freedom; she made it into represented art but left untranscribed its most vital intonations.

Hurston's authorial dualism, to put it another way, reproduces a dualism inherent in African-American expression as it evolved out of slave culture. "The white man is always trying to know into somebody else's business," she writes in *Mules and Men*, paraphrasing the theory of masking that underlies those cultural gestures and folktales intended for a white audience. "All right, I'll set something outside the door of my mind for him to play with and handle. He can read my writing but he sho' can't read my mind." In black arts and language, mimicry includes the parodic signifying on the master's culture and his language, and to that extent it assumes a position of political subordination to the dominant culture. By the same token, however, mimicry folds its object back into itself, recomposing it on its own terms and making it new—as, for instance, Charlie Parker recomposed standard popular tunes in the repertoire of jazz, creating black culture by turning mundane white materials into genius.

As my remarks on dialect have already suggested, the ground of mimicry lies in combined revelation and secrecy, the "indirection" common to theories of slave acculturation and the rise of black dialect. Because of its constant and various pressure of protection, resistance, and dissembling, slave language—the act of talking, the trope of the tongue, borne directly into work and worship songs—came to be riddled with ambiguities and defined by silence or indirection. According to Herskovits and more recent commentators, the principles of subterfuge and concealment that could be found to operate in the language of any oppressed group were strengthened in the case of black America because "indirection" was such a strong part of the language and social etiquette brought by Africans to the New World, where it was transferred, for example, into the animal or Master-John folktales, in which circumlocution and indirection are of paramount importance and constitute the allegorical substructure of the tales themselves. Sustained by a tension between violation and preservation, the "lying" sessions of the folk that Hurston placed at the heart of black communal history, when the stories of the ancestors, in slavery or in Africa, were reiterated and adorned with the verbal pyrotechnics of black talk, made dialect a reservoir of semantic resistance and cultural freedom.

The Eatonville lying sessions, which are re-created in *Mules and Men* and *Their Eyes Were Watching God*, Hurston fondly recalled in *Dust Tracks on the Road* as occasions to hear the storytellers "straining against each other in telling folks tales." Certainly not all the tales are coded with the dynamics of slavery or racial subordination, but many are, and both the alteration of the master's language into the pleasure of tall tales and the construction of allegories of subversion and rebellion employed the survival tactic of verbal economy and indirection, elevating the capacity to carry on secret communication within a disciplinary regime into an expression of culture itself. "Straining," moreover, asks us to think of the lie of the folktale in relation to the straining sounds of the work song and the sermon—the conversion of language into the sheer exertion of sound in those instances acting as a trope of striving under the economic and spiritual burden of racial subordination. Black language might itself be said to be marked by "straining," coded in an alternative sound and diction that, like the motifs of the folktales, can be printed as dialect but cannot be adequately represented by such indices. The very sign of such "straining," dialect therefore cannot be limited to orthography and syntax but includes figuration, rhythm, intonation, indirection, and silence—all the features that might constitute the art of African-American vernacular.

In his divorce trial, John Pearson refuses to testify against the infidelities of Hattie because he does not want whites to hear more about the supposed immorality of blacks: "Dey knows too much 'bout us as it is, but dey some things dey ain't tuh know." The white world, in fact, has a minimal role in the book. At the same time, of course, Hurston's translation of the autobiographical details of her parents' lives, her incorporation of black tales and folklore, and her reproduction of the Lovelace sermon required negotiating the color line between cultural worlds, telling and withholding in the same gesture. Just as she inevitably gave credence to popular folktales of the preacher's sexual prowess and privileged infidelities in the story of John Pearson, she also magnified his power as a community leader and his eloquence as a folk composer. And just as his "wounds of Jesus" sermon is a hypocritical rationalization of his own immorality, it is also an index of the very transfusion into his person of the "hammers of creation"—the artistry and labor of black America dramatized in his ritual theatrical telling of his people's history. Playing the oratorical drum of John Pearson's voice and C. C. Lovelace's sermon, Hurston held African-American vernacular art at a critical point of balance between preservation and erosion, between the transcribed and the unrecordable. She rewrote the foundational arts of slave culture in a modern idiom but left the reader—the white reader in particular, but perhaps the black as well—with an admonition: "He can read my writing but he sho' can't read my mind."

THREE

"A Song without Words":
Black Thunder

Let us consider two inflammatory passages:

> Like a cancer, eating into the vitals of Alabama law and order,
> this tirade is being driven into the heart and the brain of the
> negro with the hope that it will ignite the spark of savagery that
> once controlled the instincts of his ancestors and send him
> tearing at the throat of the white man.

> It is evident that the French principles of liberty and equality
> have been infused into the minds of the Negroes and that the
> incautious and intemperate use of the words by some whites
> among us have inspired them with confidence. . . . While the
> fiery Hotspurs of the State vociferate their French babble of the
> natural equality of man, the insulted Negro will be constantly
> stimulated to cast away his cords and to sharpen his pike.

The second passage comes from *Black Thunder*, Arna Bontemps's
1938 masterpiece of historical meditation. The language is borrowed from contemporary newspapers that attributed Gabriel's
thwarted 1800 slave uprising in Richmond, Virginia, to the subversive stimulation of French Revolutionary propaganda, which

had been raised to a pitch by the black rebellion in San Domingo under the leadership of Toussaint L'Ouverture. The first passage, to which we will return, is comparable to the second in its attribution of African-American desires for liberty and equality to the effects of outside agitation. It is possibly more modern in its language, but, if anything, is less temperate in tone.

In an essay-length memoir of the Harlem Renaissance, Bontemps recalled the effervescent period of the late 1920s as the "golden days" that were about to be shattered by economic ruin. He remembered that the glittering reception he received in 1931 upon the publication of his first novel, *God Sends Sunday*, put him in mind of a "legendary people of antiquity pleasuring themselves and celebrating as their cities were about to be destroyed." Soon, he added, he himself would turn to pensive short stories on racial themes and to "brooding over a subject matter so depressing that [he] could find no relief until it resolved itself as *Black Thunder*." Bontemps's indirection here may be taken to exemplify the indirection that the novel itself practiced, probing history for its repetitions and layers, its failure to lay old ghosts to rest. The depressing subject matter that obsessed him in the early 1930s was Scottsboro. Moving to Huntsville, Alabama, as the spendthrift glory of pre-Depression Harlem collapsed, Bontemps moved into the world of the folk, from whom he had been separated and who now, under even more severe economic necessity, were returning to the land, rediscovering the "woods and swamps and streams with which their ancestors had been intimate a century earlier and about which their grandparents still talked wistfully." In addition, he moved straight into a contemporary travesty of justice that would come to stand for American racism at its most dismaying— despite the assertion of pride on the part of Alabama authorities that they had finally transcended the rule of Judge Lynch—and into a consequent personal crisis that resolved itself through a reexamination of one of the signal events in antebellum black history.

Driven from Alabama by the turmoil surrounding the Scottsboro trials, Bontemps moved back to Los Angeles, where he had been raised after his birth in Louisiana. Now married, he lived once again with his parents long enough to complete *Black Thunder* before setting out for Chicago and a continuation of his career as an eminent writer of African-American biographies, children's books, anthologies of poetry and folklore, history, and fiction. Because his fictional work has never had a large following, the great scope of Bontemps's career has often been overlooked, but few writers produced quality work in so many genres, most notably in historical biography for general audiences and younger readers. He received a degree in library science in 1943 and later took a position as librarian at Fisk University, where he built one of the most important collections of African-American materials in the country. Such work in preserving the history of African Americans—in fact, in giving them a public voice at all—was already reflected with great passion in *Black Thunder*.

The "cancer eating into the vitals of Alabama law and order" and "driven into the heart and brain of the negro," leading him to acts of atavistic savagery, as the first passage argued, was Communism, and the quotation comes from a book published in Alabama at the time of the Scottsboro case. Because of the International Labor Defense's opportunistic takeover of the Scottsboro case, Communism in some quarters came to be seen as the source of any such contraventions of southern law, any disturbances in the delicate racial equilibrium that segregation, it was said, guaranteed. In this instance, however, Communism was sometimes only a code word for northern liberalism, or more generally for the spectre of "outside" interference in southern affairs. In a notorious essay, the prominent southern historian Frank Owsley called Scottsboro the "Third Crusade; the Sequel to Abolitionism and Reconstruction." Like Reconstruction, which resulted in "the most abominable phase barbarism had assumed since the dawn of civilization," when northern radicals had encouraged blacks to "commit universal pillage, murder and rape," said Owsley, agitation on behalf of the "Scottsboro boys," as they were characteristically called by both sides, could only lead to violent southern retaliation.

The parallels between Gabriel's rising and the case of the Scottsboro defendants are hardly exact. But Scottsboro was Bontemps's point of departure and provided the framework in which he reimagined an earlier miscarriage of racial justice. In the case of Scottsboro, unlike Gabriel's rebellion, the inflammatory propaganda of Communism was not held directly responsible for the crimes the young men were said to have committed, although the sometimes easy blurring of important distinctions between the Communist party and other groups, such as the NAACP, active on behalf of the Scottsboro defendants made racist charges scattershot and easily generalized. By fastening itself parasitically to the Scottsboro case, the Communist party gave credence to the claim that it stirred up race hatred and made it easy for some southerners to vilify the defense of purported Negro rapists by "Jew money from New York" (as the prosecutor put it in his closing remarks at one trial). And, like the charges brought against Republicans and French sympathizers in postcolonial Virginia, the easy vilification of Communism obscured the basic fact that African Americans might desire freedom and equality on their own, organize and act on their own, and draw philosophical support from the fundamental ideology of American democracy—in essence be governed by the same principles of natural rights and liberty as white Americans. Not so much because of the charges brought against the young men, which were spurious enough given the evidence, but because of the mockery of justice that followed, Scottsboro appeared to prove that little had changed through the Civil War, Reconstruction, and the rise of Jim Crow. The thwarted black rebellion more than one hundred years past thus became the means for Bontemps to examine the depressing spectacle of the Scottsboro trial through the deflecting screen of historical research and imagination. He countered the common run of post-Reconstruction historiography and popular myth—which doubted that African Americans were fit for political, legal, and economic rights; and he offered a profound meditation on the fact that the need for African-American resistance to white racism had hardly lessened since Gabriel himself stood trial.

Both Scottsboro and Gabriel's rising, as Bontemps portrayed it, turn upon the law and therefore upon the political power of language broadly construed. The battle over the Scottsboro defendants was, from one perspective, a rhetorical and linguistic battle: the courts (and much of the press, especially in the South) rendered guilty verdicts and capital sentences that flew in the face of undeniable exonerating evidence and testimony. They did so by either ignoring testimonial language or making it mean what it did not say, and by allowing the corrosive language of racial mythology—the "rape complex" that set the most incredible words of any white woman above each and every word spoken by, or in defense of, a black man—to substitute for the truth. In the case of Gabriel's rising, on the contrary, there is no doubt that a "crime" was committed—that is to say, that slaveholding law was breached in a marked and terrifying way. Although the rebellion crumbled, a large-scale, well-concealed conspiracy against the slaveholding regime certainly did exist. As in the case of Scottsboro, however, its public meaning was adjudicated through the language of the masters—their courts, their press, and their government. The testimony of blacks had no meaning except to a handful of abolitionists and later curious historians, few of whom considered the near revolt more than a minor event and none of whom would begin to examine such events from the perspective of vernacular slave culture until a full generation after Bontemps's novel was written.

The Scottsboro case bears on *Black Thunder* in several key respects yet to be examined, but Bontemps's superimposition of the two historical moments may be estimated in his description of Gabriel drifting off into dreamy meditation as the prosecutor drones on about the incomprehensibility of "well-kept slaves" turning suddenly into "mad dogs." Bontemps writes: "Gabriel felt the scene withdrawing. . . . Further and further away it receded. Again there was that insulting mockery of words he could not understand, that babble of legal language and political innuendo. . . . Demons. Freedom. Deviltry. Justice. Funny words. All of them sounded like conjure now." Surely the Scottsboro defendants, more than a century later, felt even less confidence in the language of American justice. In inventing Gabriel's courtroom testimony, but moreover in designing his novel to recreate the conspiracy from the African-American point of view, Bontemps explored both the power and the limits of language in a contradictory world of both great political freedom and racial totalization.

* * *

In comparing the language of law to conjure, Bontemps defines Gabriel and his aborted conspiracy from a peculiar angle, for although conjure has undeniable power in the slave world recreated in *Black Thunder*, it is set in contrast to the decidedly rational foundation provided for Gabriel's bid to be free. Conjure operates as an instrument of retribution against those slaves who betray the conspirators' plans; but its relationship to the failure of the plot is ambivalent. The novel's narrative, of course, is circumscribed to a great degree by the historical facts that Bontemps gathered in part from the *Calendar of Virginia State Papers* for 1799–1807, among other sources, and his challenge was to make plausible, but not pitiable, the disintegration of the conspiracy from both within (by betrayal, fear, and "superstition") and without (by one of the largest storms in recent Virginia history). When other slaves interpret the mammoth rainstorm that sweeps in just as the uprising gets underway as an ill omen, even the sign of conjure, Gabriel defies those who "talk about signs" and fear a "bad hand" has been set against the rebels. Nonetheless, in the novel as in historical fact, the storm dissuades many from carrying out the planned rebellion, and along with the betrayal by trusted slaves it destroys any chance of success. Bontemps's title itself is of course divided between these possibilities: "black thunder" refers on one hand to the heroic defiance of the rebels, and on the other to the intervening natural event that crushes the rebellion and that was considered by some whites, who believed in their own form of conjure, to have been "providential." In the aftermath of the rebellion's collapse, an old slave woman tells Juba, Gabriel's lover, that the "stars wasn't right" and that the rebels spent too much time "listening to Mingo read a white man's book"—the Bible—whereas Toussaint and his followers, she claims, "kilt a hog in the woods [and] drank the blood."

Like Denmark Vesey after him, Toussaint appears to have employed elements of conjure in rousing the slaves of San Domingo; but like Gabriel, he was a man whose thought was permeated by the principles of the Age of Revolution. If the only role of conjure in *Black Thunder* were to explain the failure of the mass of slaves to join the rebellion, however, it would be incidental at best. Instead, it is part of Bontemps's searching attempt to recover the meaning of the insurrection from a variegated African-American point of view that could include Gabriel's astute articulation of revolutionary political ideals as well as a folk understanding of the spiritual basis for freedom. Sympathetic accounts of the African-American right to rebel were certainly available to Bontemps—for example, in Thomas Wentworth Higginson's seminal article "Gabriel's Defeat," which appeared first along with his companion pieces on Denmark Vesey and Nat Turner in the *Atlantic Monthly* in 1862 (all of them later collected in the 1889 volume *Travellers and Outlaws*) and from which Bontemps borrowed heavily. But no one, no historian and no novelist, had written so completely of the motives and barriers to revolt as though from within slave culture.

The significance of this strand in the novel is illuminated by a passage in Bontemps's later essay about the South, "Why I Returned." Recalling in 1965 the contrary attitudes toward black folklore and folk wisdom taken by his father, a modern skeptic, and his great-uncle Buddy, a believer, Bontemps placed the issue in the context of his own education at San Fernando Academy, an all-white boarding school near Los Angeles, and later at Pacific Union College:

In their opposing attitudes toward roots my father and my great-uncle made me aware of a conflict in which every educated American Negro, and some who are not educated, must somehow take sides. By implication at least, one group advocates embracing the riches of the folk heritage; their opposites demand a clean break with the past and all it represents. Had I not gone home summers and hob-nobbed with folk-type Negroes, I would have finished college without knowing that any Negro other than Paul Laurence Dunbar ever wrote a poem. I would have come out imagining that the story of the Negro could be told in two short paragraphs: a statement about jungle people in Africa and an equally brief account of the slavery issue in

American history. The reserves of human vitality that enabled the race to survive the worst of both these experiences while at the same time making contributions to western culture remained a dark secret with my teachers, if they had considered the matter at all. I was given no inkling by them, and my white classmates who needed to know such things as much as I did if we were to maintain a healthy regard for each other in the future, were similarly denied.

Telling the story of Gabriel's revolt from inside out and from the bottom up, as well as from the perspective of the masters' historical record, *Black Thunder* dramatically includes the "reserves of human vitality" that have so often been ignored or censored in the narrative of American culture. However skeptical Bontemps expects his reader to be about conjure or "signs" as an explanation of the rebellion's failure, his extensive use of folk belief is a means to put the language of the masters and the language of the slaves on a continuum and to discover in the coded discourse of vernacular an equivalent to the philosophical language of the Rights of Man. At critical junctures, as in the case of the black sermonic language examined previously in chapter 2, the folk language of *Black Thunder* bypasses the verbal and moves into the domain of tonality. To a great degree, Gabriel's "rational" language of liberty remains ascendant in the novel, just as the legal discourse of the slaveholders summarily distinguishes between freedom and sedition; but the whispering, singing, humming, and silent language of the slaves runs in a remarkable undercurrent throughout the entire text, giving a special voice to those whose testimony, in court and in history, had been accorded no legal or official historical meaning.

The central moments in this regard come early on, and one could even call them the climax of the novel, since the spiritual truth of the rebellion lies in the conspiracy itself rather than in the revolt that never comes to pass. Building on the fact that Gabriel was known to have employed religious meetings as occasions for recruiting followers in his plot (one of his most important meetings followed the funeral of a child, where he announced his intention "to fight for his Country"), Bontemps creates a series of linked scenes that make slave worship, as the site of an intersection between African retentions and Christian radicalism, a cover for conspiracy. When Ben Woolfolk, the slave of Moseley Sheppard who will ultimately betray the conspiracy, is asked to swear his allegiance, Gabriel's brother presents him with icons of that syncretism: "Here's the Book [the Bible], and here's the pot of blood, and here's the black-cat bone. Swear." Ben's swearing takes place at the funeral of Bundy, the old slave beaten to death by Gabriel's master, Thomas Prosser, and the one who has exacted from Ben his fatal promise to join the black "freemasons"— a code word for the seditious influence of French Revolutionary politics yoked now to promised black insurrection. Bundy's funeral is a virtual catalogue of African survivals, from the burial practices, to the ceremonial singing, to the belief in Bundy's spirit commanding Ben to swear: "something—something no denser than smoke—squatting by the hole, grinning pleasantly with one eye on the jug of rum." The mourners, Bontemps says, "remembered Africa in 1800," and one particular sign of that remembrance lies in their singing: "They had raised a song without words. They were kneeling with their faces to the sun. Their hands in the air, the fingers apart, and they bowed and rose together as they sang. Up came the songs like a wave, and down went their faces in the dirt. . . . The black folks, some of them naked to the waist, kept bowing to the sun, bowing and rising as they sang. Their arms quivered above their heads. . . . Ben knelt down and joined the song, moaning with the others at the place where the two worlds meet." The liminal terrain where two worlds meet is both that between life and death and that between American and Africa (or between Christianity and African spiritualism), a confluence relatively common in slave worship and in some spirituals. But the "song without words," the wailing, moaning, sonorous murmur or hum—"Lord, Lord. Mm-mm-mm-mm"—stands also on a boundary between language and sound that reappears throughout *Black Thunder*, signifying the complex implication of words, speech, and writing in the quest for liberty, as well as the subcultural text of slave language that stands inherently in a relation of concealed dissent and subversion to the language of the masters. Like the hum of the African-American sermon or the spirituals in their most intense moments of transport—the vocalism that makes the rendering of dialect and the transcription of song so difficult— the hum of the mourners likewise moves language into a sacred dimension of tonality and allies it to the murmuring, whispering, and otherwise secretive communication that defines the slaves' conspiracy over the course of the novel.

For Bontemps's purposes, the African retentions are a crucial counterweight to the political and religious world of the masters; by the same token, however, they are not presented as the direct source of insurrectionary ideology. The funeral, in fact, seems to contain neither a Christian nor a secular political dimension at all until Gabriel counsels the mourners to "hush moaning" and recall Mingo's previous reading of scripture as a call to arms against the masters. On that occasion Mingo had read a wild litany of scriptural passages—from Exodus, Jeremiah, Psalms, Isaiah, Ezekial, Matthew, Proverbs, James, and Malachi—authorizing resistance to bondage and prophesying the Lord's judgment upon the oppressors. Accompanying Mingo's reading is the choric call-and-response of the gathered people that allies articulated tonality to the summoning of resistant power: "The Negroes murmured audibly, but they made no words." In seizing Mingo's oration as a text of revolution, Gabriel pinpoints scripture as a pragmatic tool that can mediate between his own rationalist philosophy and the sequestering folk beliefs of the other slaves. At the same time, Bontemps demonstrates that Christianity can act as a cloak for resistance: when Thomas Prosser interrupts the plotting taking place at Bundy's funeral, the slaves quickly return to their song, "the same swaying of bodies, the same shouts punctuating the song." In small compass, then, the funeral outlines the relationship between black religion and a politics of resistance on the southern plantation.

Even though no univocal interpretation of the role of resistance in slave religion is possible, Bontemps clearly falls on the side that argues for a strong nurturing of political radicalism within the practices of Afro-Christianity. Clandestine religious meetings in the slave community offered more than simply an opportunity to interpret the Bible free from the often hypocritical teachings of the institutional church or missionaries, or to escape from the harsh daily realities of oppression. If it strains the evidence to designate all such services "African cult" meetings, as have a few historians, slave worship without question forged communal bonds that often remained invisible to planters—or called forth surveillance and suppression because of their fear of conspiracy and insurrection, especially in the wake of the revolt in San Domingo. Taking place in a cabin or in an outdoor "hush harbor" sometimes considered to have sacred or magical properties, the slaves' prayer meeting brought together Christian and African forms of worship and connected American blacks to an ancestral past through syncretic performance of song and dance, or the reiteration of ancestral burial practices such as the ones outlined by Bontemps. That is to say, Christianity itself could provide a mechanism for the continuation of African practices like the ring shout and the antiphonal call-and-response of the spirituals. As Sterling Stuckey observes, "The very features of Christianity peculiar to slaves were often outward manifestations of deeper African religious concerns, products of a religious outlook toward which the master class might otherwise be hostile." In addition, however, the contended language of Christian worship could provide the very language of slave resistance, whether in the form of the spirituals, which were often laden with messages of rebellion (even if combined with accommodation), or in antinomian interpretations of the Bible.

It is clear that slave religion, certainly when it was presided over by white ministers but also at times when practiced within the more protected confines of black worship, acted partially to control rebelliousness and at times to instill docile passivity in the face of hopeless odds. But the counsel of patience and Christian submission could not entirely silence the revolutionary message of biblical prophecy. Those who acted to suppress slave worship understood that the Bible itself, as the language of the spirituals eloquently demonstrated, could become the vehicle of what would today be called a liberation theology. The powerful example of the leadership of Moses and the Israelite delivery from bondage, the admonitions and jeremiads of the Old Testament prophets, and the forecast of the New Jerusalem all provided a strong counterweight to Jesus' redemption—or else were seen to be realized in the Passion—and often constituted the heart of slave religion, particularly when it became interwoven, as in the spirituals, with the political language of revolution. As Nat Turner's case makes abundantly evident, moreover, the centrality of the gospels to slave worship, as promoted by the masters, could hardly guarantee pacifistic subservience. Turner identified with Christ as the final revolutionary prophet even as he plotted his revolt for the Fourth of July. But as in the case of many slaves, the majority according to some observers, his own inspiration by-passed the New Testament teaching that slaveholders preferred and derived instead from the scriptures of prophecy and the apocalypse: Turner is reputed to have preached in the last sermon before his 1831 rising from the text of Revelation. Like Gabriel and more so Nat Turner, Denmark Vesey also exploited prayer meetings and biblical prophecy in organizing his conspiracy, in particular by reading passages from the Bible, one conspirator later testified, *"where God commanded, that all should be cut off, both men, women, and children,"* and the community hysteria that followed each exposed conspiracy frequently focused on the purported blasphemy and profanity of the slaves' misinterpretation of scripture. For example, the court that sentenced Denmark Vesey and ten of his conspirators to death pointedly quoted the Pauline scripture most often cited by slaveholders (*"Servants, obey in all things your masters . . ."*), even though such a citation risked being understood as rank hypocrisy or taken over and made an instrument of resistance by slaves. Witness Nat Turner's own citation of Luke 12:47 in his "Confessions": "For he who knoweth his Master's will, and doeth it not, shall be beaten with many stripes, and thus have I chastened you." Here Turner appropriated and overturned one of proslavery's favorite passages, transfiguring a text of racist subjugation into his own prophetic call to revolt. For many slaveholders the scripture was a tool of suppression; for Turner, as for Gabriel, it became the weapon of God's own violent chastening of the masters.

Gerald Mullin has speculated that Gabriel's rebellion failed in part because it lacked a sacred dimension on the order of Turner's (or even that of Vesey, who employed a conjure man to help arouse his followers). However, given the size of Gabriel's following and the extent of the conspiracy, kept secret for months preceding the abortive rising, it seems more likely that the storm and betrayals account for the failure. (In addition, Turner's group was much smaller and apparently had no grand strategy beyond local terror—hardly a strategy to discount but in any case one apparently less sophisticated than Gabriel's.) In Gabriel's case the sacred dimension was complexly interwoven with the secular. If it was less overtly millenarian than Turner's vision, Gabriel's was nonetheless capable of integrating Afro-Christian beliefs into its political framework. Even so, Bontemps's version of the conspiracy in *Black Thunder* does suggest that the rural black folk moved in a world that Gabriel could understand but from which he had detached himself intellectually. Those two worlds are clearly bifurcated at the end of the novel, with the hero Gabriel and the traitor Ben Woolfolk going to their separate punishments. Gabriel, it was later testified, had intended to drape himself in a silk flag on which was to be written the phrase "death or liberty." Although he took inspiration from Moses and the prophets and recognized the power of scripture and Afro-Christian religion as a means of organization, Gabriel's own Bible was American.

• • •

Or was it French? Bontemps's first chapter is titled simply "Jacobins." In the postcolonial struggle over the meaning of America between the Federalists and the Republicans, the charge of "Jacobinism" frequently carried as a subtext the charge of inciting slave rebellion, despite the fact that few Republicans, certainly not the 1800 presidential candidate Thomas Jefferson, advocated immediate emancipation, much less violent black revolution. The central point of reference in reiterated fears of Jacobin conspiracy among slaves and abolitionists, on through the Civil War, was the revolt in San Domingo, where the outbreak of revolution in 1791 under the leadership of Toussaint had sent a flood of white planter refugees to the United States, many of them carrying both slaves and tales of terror to the South. Following the achievement of independence in 1804, and then again especially in the wake of Nat Turner's uprising in 1831 and the emancipation of slaves in British Jamaica in the same year, San Domingo seemed the fearful precursor of black rebellion throughout the New World, becoming an immutable feature of master class ideology in both Latin America and the United States. In the wake of Vesey's near revolt in 1822, Charleston editor Edwin C. Holland called for the vigorous suppression of slaves and warned his readers not to forget that "our Negroes are truely [sic] the *Jacobins* of the country; that they are the *anarchists* and the *domestic enemy;* the *common enemy of civilized society,* and the barbarians who would, if they could, become the destroyers *of our race.*"

As *Black Thunder* makes evident, the same might well have been feared of Gabriel's conspiracy. Relying on the historical record in most important respects, Bontemps portrays Jacobinism less as a cause of the conspiracy than as the ideological context in which it came to maturity. In detailing the Federalists' manipulation of the rebellion and subsequent public fears in their propaganda war against Jefferson; in citing the accusations made against Republican polemicist James Thomson Callender (named Thomas Callender in the novel), already jailed under the Sedition Act, that he helped plot the insurrection; in weaving into his plot the stories of two Frenchmen, Charles Quersey and Alexander Beddenhurst (their parts variously rewritten for Creuzot and Biddenhurst), known to have been involved in the conspiracy; and in ranging Gabriel's philosophy of natural rights against the countersubversive attacks on the incendiary work of the Amis des Noirs and the revolutionary cataclysm in San Domingo—by all such historical details Bontemps meticulously re-creates the atmosphere in which both white masters *and* black slaves lived in turn-of-the-century Virginia.

The "strange music" of liberty, equality, fraternity that Gabriel overhears in an early scene near Creuzot's printing shop—words that give him gooseflesh, "words for things that had been in his mind, things that he didn't know had names"—provides motive and form for Gabriel's inchoate ideas. The intellectual coherence of *Black Thunder*, in fact, lies to a good extent in its careful integration of Revolutionary politics and slave subversion, its careful construction of a framework of white Republican or French radicalism that can accommodate, without crudely producing, an African-American philosophy of natural rights, and therefore in its assertion that the two ideological worlds are continuous, not contradictory. Like the rebellion of Nat Turner a generation later, the conspiracy of Gabriel occurred at a moment of considerable debate about the possibility of gradual emancipation, notably adumbrated in St. George Tucker's *A Dissertation on Slavery* (1796), a work to which Bontemps explicitly alludes. Along with an economic and political turn against such theories, in the North as well as the South, Gabriel's conspiracy, like Turner's revolt, hardened sentiment against abolition. Nevertheless, neither the philosophical right to revolution nor the slave's claim to it would disappear. As Tucker's cousin George Tucker wrote in an 1803 pamphlet advocating the colonization of blacks to an area west of the Mississippi (a plan debated by the Virginia legislature in *Black Thunder* in the wake of Gabriel's arrest): "Every year adds to the number of those who can read and write; and he who has made any proficiency in letters, becomes a little centre of instruction to others. This increase of knowledge is the principal agent in evolving the spirit we have to fear. The love of freedom, sir, is an inborn sentiment, which the God of nature has planted deep in the heart. . . . This celestial spark, which fires the breast of the savage, which glows in that of the philosopher, is not extinguished in the bosom of the slave. It may be buried in the embers; but it still lives; and the breath of knowledge kindles it into flame. Thus we find, sir, there never have been slaves in any country, who have not seized the first favorable opportunity to revolt." John Randolph, witnessing the rebels in custody, more bluntly declared that they exhibited "a sense of their rights, and contempt of danger, and a thirst for revenge" that, if they were to become general among the slaves, "must deluge the Southern country in blood."

In placing him in a politically charged context and showing him to be inspired by the Rights of Man, however, Bontemps by no means diminishes Gabriel's own intellect. For one thing, Bontemps critiques the very clear limits of white perceptions of African-American political consciousness, and he ridicules Biddenhurst and other such fair-weather abolitionists for having the luxury to flee town while Gabriel's band must stand and die as slaves. (Along with the sometimes telltale anachronistic language of modern proletarian revolution ascribed to the French radicals in *Black Thunder*, details of this sort serve as well to extend Bontemps's scrutiny of those white supporters of the Scottsboro defendants who, however fine their motives and their work, also had the luxury of returning north rather than going to prison or the electric chair.) If Gabriel's political philosophy is symbiotic in formation and articulation, it nonetheless belongs, in its origins, to his own, or his community's, black consciousness. What sets him to "thinking about how [he]'d like to be free" comes as much from within as from without, a fact Bontemps later underlined in his 1968 preface to the novel when he referred to the revolt as an act of "self-emancipation." I make this point because it would be easy but misleading to assume that Bontemps's historicity obscures Gabriel's independence of thought. Like Frederick Douglass in recounting his own life or dramatizing that of Madison Washington in his short story "The Heroic Slave," Bontemps chose to make

Gabriel an American first, a black slave second, much as Toussaint considered himself a Frenchman rather than an African. Like Douglass, Bontemps chose to dwell on the "right of revolution" denied to slaves in such court cases as those concerning revolts aboard the slave ships *Amistad* and *Creole*, asserting that natural law transcended the rule of slavery. This is clearest, perhaps, in Bontemps's most pronounced deviation from fact in the novel, Gabriel's courtroom testimony, which brings to a climax the deployment of political language in *Black Thunder*. But the interplay between the world of the slaves and the world of the masters also puts Jacobinism to another use—namely, to tie Gabriel to a network of political radicalism commensurate with the sophistication and breadth of his vision.

Although Bontemps did not explore Gabriel's exact rationale for the revolt or have available the facts that are now more evident, a few further details are worth notice. The conspiracy itself, which could conceivably have led to the largest slave rebellion in United States history, was both remarkably astute and deeply flawed. Douglas Egerton's thorough study of Gabriel's rising in light of the turmoil surrounding the elections of 1800 demonstrates conclusively that Gabriel had a well-formulated, if naive, strategy, rooted in abstract notions of democratic liberty with a practical goal. Close to half of Richmond's population was black, and one-fifth of these were free. Like many in his immediate cohort, Gabriel was a skilled and literate artisan, part of a relatively elite, assimilated class of urban slaves who were conversant with politics and economics. As a skilled blacksmith, Gabriel seldom worked as a field hand and was occasionally allowed to hire his own time in Richmond. This comparative "freedom," Egerton persuasively shows, led Gabriel to conceive of slave liberty as not just a philosophical but also an economic issue. Gabriel wanted to keep his earnings, and he sought to join the problem of slavery to what he perceived to be a class war between artisans and merchants, thereby exploiting the larger struggle between Federalists and Republicans, who were ascendant everywhere in Virginia except in the Federalist strongholds targeted by the rebellion—principally Richmond, but also Petersburg and Norfolk. Clearly, however, Gabriel's sophistication had a limit. Following a guerilla strike against Richmond's warehouse district and capitol, during which unsympathetic whites would be killed indiscriminately as a show of force through terror, the initial band of some two hundred men planned to take Governor James Monroe hostage. With Richmond fortified, Gabriel apparently believed, many among the city's white working class, the predominantly Republican planters in the surrounding countryside, and the large population of rural slaves would be inspired to join the rebellion, thus making it possible for the rebels to negotiate their freedom and the right to participate as equals in the Virginia economy.

It is nearly inconceivable that such white, Republican support would have arisen in the course of any slave insurrection, and the rural slave population, far more of whom were native African or children of Africans, had not been sufficiently integrated into the political goals envisioned by Gabriel's group, despite the fact that secret knowledge of the plot had been successfully spread throughout a large area of Virginia, reaching as far away as Charlottesville and Norfolk. In any event, Bontemps did not attempt to speculate about the exact reasoning behind the plot, relying instead on a broad articulation of Revolutionary doctrine. But he thereby added a most crucial element, one that seems to be little in evidence, except by implication, in the records of the conspiracy and its suppression. Casting a stark shadow over Gabriel's planned insurrection in *Black Thunder* is the contemporary slave revolution in San Domingo. The novel's first intimation of the conspiracy occurs in an oblique conversation between Gabriel and

General John on the wharf where a ship from San Domingo has just docked; and among the crowd gathered near the conclusion to witness Gabriel's transfer from Norfolk to Richmond is a black sailor from San Domingo of whom Bontemps writes: "He had seen Dessalines ride a horse. He knew the sight of Christophe. He understood now that words like *freedom* and *liberty* drip blood— always, everywhere, there was blood on such words. Still he'd like to see this Gabriel. Was he as tall as Christophe, as broad as Dessalines? Was he as stern-faced as Toussaint, the tiger?"

What Bontemps specifically adds to the historical context, that is to say, is an invocation of *black* Revolutionary inspiration, a narrative strategy that at once puts Gabriel's plot on a more complex—and no doubt a more historically accurate—plane while at the same time setting aside its impracticality. By linking Gabriel's rebellion to that in San Domingo, Bontemps asks us to understand that the achievement of its actual objectives, in this case implausible, need not be the only measure of "success" in slave resistance. Understood in terms of its destruction and inspired terror, Nat Turner's insurrection was highly successful; Gabriel's conspiracy, like those of Vesey and others, embodied heroism, dignity, spiritual character, and political wisdom even as it failed, at the final moment, to materialize. Set against the example of San Domingo, which Bontemps would take up in his far less compelling next novel, *Drums at Dusk* (1938), Gabriel's conspiracy may seem all the more unworkable, but it must also be seen as all the more exemplary of the fact that postcolonial American slaves saw themselves acting in the Revolutionary epoch.

Toussaint's name echoes throughout *Black Thunder*—as it did in much abolitionist literature and in virtually every antebellum text of African-American resistance—to the point that Bontemps even invents a letter from Toussaint calling on American slaves to join their cause to his own: "*I have undertaken to avenge your wrongs. It is my desire that liberty and equality shall reign. I am striving to this end. Come and unite with us, brothers, and combat with us for the same cause.*" The letter is important in several respects: it puts United States slavery in a New World context, as Melville did in *Benito Cereno* and Martin Delany in *Blake*; it suggests that Gabriel's own strategy, well organized and articulated, may have had a hemispheric, *black* dimension and, at any rate, had an inspiration distinct from local white radicalism; and it casts Gabriel, despite the relative "failure" of his rising, in the role of nationalist hero. To invoke Toussaint was to lay bare the paradoxical way in which slavery and revolution were linked throughout antebellum history. Acclaimed by abolitionists, white and black alike—but also, in the first decades of the century, by some southern supporters of slavery as well, who rightly considered him dignified, compassionate, and economically conservative—Toussaint belonged to the great age of the founding fathers and should rightly have stood beside them as an ancestral hero. When he compared Toussaint in an 1854 lecture not only to Nat Turner ("the Spartacus of the Southampton revolt") but also, as had Garrison and others, to Napoleon and Washington, William Wells Brown underscored the withering irony that, whereas Washington's government "enacted laws by which chains were fastened upon the limbs of millions of people," Toussaint's "made liberty its watchword, incorporated it in its constitution, abolished the slave trade, and made freedom universal amongst the people."

By the time of Brown's lecture on San Domingo, subtitled "Its Revolutions and Its Patriots," Gabriel himself was considered one of the *African American* fathers of American freedom, cited by Brown, Douglass, Delany, Henry Highland Garnet, and other black leaders as a heroic model on a par with the white founding fathers, and it is likely that Bontemps in his research for *Black Thunder* came across the testimony from one of the conspirators that ran: "I have nothing more to offer than what General Washington would have had to offer, had he been taken by the British and put to trial. I have adventured my life in endeavouring to obtain the liberty of my countrymen, and am a willing sacrifice in their cause." Whether or not he knew this document, Bontemps followed the tradition established by black antebellum writers—Douglass's "The Heroic Slave" is the preeminent example—of tying slave revolution to the moral principles of the Age of Revolution and making African-American access to the language of liberty a primary trope.

. . .

Black Thunder is permeated by a circulation of texts: political pamphlets, scripture, laws, historical documents, conspiratorial talk, propaganda, incendiary and incriminating letters, rumors, portents and signs, whispering and hushing, sounds figuratively indicative of natural rights (the singing of birds, the chattering of squirrels, the tremor of the earth), songs, moaning and humming, and even defiant silence—this whole panoply of linguistic signs indicating a rigidly hierarchical human universe nonetheless striated by rebellious discourse and messages of natural freedom that challenge the rule of slavery. The entire text is a network of completed, forestalled, and punished communications, of linguistic subversion and countersubversion, and Bontemps's careful fluctuation between the worlds of slave and master makes historicism a means of recovering the "subtext" of African America, from the grand leadership of Toussaint to the vernacular of the slave quarters. The semiotic structure of the book has the effect, in particular, of creating a historical voice for the slaves—placing their lives into the documentary record from which they had been excluded and, at the time Bontemps wrote in the 1930s, redressing the reigning historiographical account of slaves and black freedmen alike as unfit for equality. Between the intersecting worlds of master and slave stands the testimony of Gabriel, which is the epitome of Bontemps's various linkages between language and liberty, and which speaks as forcefully to the decimation of African-American rights in the age of Scottsboro as to the crisis in postcolonial political philosophy. A further means of connecting the two superimposed eras may be found in the figure of Juba, Gabriel's lover, to whom Bontemps gives a prominent but, at first glance, vexing role.

Beyond question, one of the most riveting scenes in the book is Thomas Prosser's whipping of Juba, whose heroism is at every point depicted as equal to Gabriel's. In the wake of Gabriel's capture, Juba shirks field labor, and when challenged by Prosser her defiance is purposely linguistic in nature. In answer to his demand to know how much tobacco she has cut, Juba responds: "You talking to me, Marse Prosser?" The brutal whipping that he proceeds to give her takes the form of a triangulated tableau. Although her "thighs [are] raw like cut beef and bloody," Juba refuses to speak, even to flinch under the lash, only throwing "a swift, hateful glance at the powerful man pouring the hot melted lead on her flesh." As it becomes wet with blood, Prosser's whip itself begins to speak, as it were, "making words like *sa-lack, sa-lack, sa-lack* as it twined around [Juba's] thin hips." Interspersed between Juba's silent defiance and Prosser's overtly sexualized whipping of Juba with her raised petticoats is the "dove-like lamentation" of the surrounding chorus of slaves: "Pray, massa, pray. Oh, pray, massa."

Juba is ruined as a slave, and in the final episode of the novel Ben will see her on the auction block. This economical and stunning scene of punishment constitutes Bontemps's most pointed critique of slave subservience—not Juba's, of course, but that registered in the choral lament that accompanies the scene. The chant of "Pray, massa. Oh, pray, massa," is intended both to plea for mercy on Juba and to convey the damnation Prosser and all such slaveholders bring upon themselves (Bontemps may have borrowed the chant from a comparable scene of whipping that William Wells Brown recalled in his 1880 volume, *My Southern Home*). Yet it is a decidedly pallid message in light of Juba's stoic assertion that she will no longer be a slave in spirit. Because of the stylized sado-eroticism of the scene, one is tempted to compare the whipping of Juba to the famous whipping of his Aunt Esther in Frederick Douglass's autobiographies, which some recent readers have seen to betray a form of male voyeurism that links the observing Douglass as much to Aaron Anthony as to Esther. Bontemps's scene is similarly voyeuristic—the more so given the way in which Juba is portrayed from the outset of the novel—but it finds a better analogy in Douglass's own rise to manhood in his famous resistance to the slavebreaker Covey. Juba does not defeat Prosser physically; but, like Douglass, she will never again be a slave, except in physical form, and her resistance is every bit as powerful, and her silence as replete with the sounds of freedom, as Gabriel's refusal to utter final words at his execution: "Let the rope talk, suh."

The "*sa-lack, sa-lack*" of Prosser's phallic whip merges sexual domination and simple brutality. Because it can elicit no cry from Juba, however, its provocative power is overwhelmed by her resistant power. From this perspective, the overt sexualization of the scene is important to the rendering of Juba's defiance. Such a reading is relevant not least because Juba is portrayed throughout the novel in problematic ways. From beginning to end she is the "tempestuous brown wench," and virtually every mention of her, most of all as Gabriel's lover, is eroticized in some way. It would be easy to dismiss this strategy as a sign of Bontemps's conventional sexism; that may play a part, but it is apparent also that Bontemps intends Juba's sexuality to be an unusual sign of freedom. The obvious example is Juba's riding of the black colt Araby, while wearing Prosser's riding boots, which Gabriel has designated as the signal that the gathering of slaves for the rebellion is to begin: "She sat astride Araby's bare back, her fragmentary skirt curled about her waist, her naked thighs flashing above the riding boots, leaned forward till her face was almost touching the wild mane and felt the warm body of the colt straining between her clinched knees. . . . Juba heard the footfalls now, heard the sweet muffled clatter on the hardened earth and her breathing became quick and excited. It occurred to her benumbed mind that she was giving the sign." Why Bontemps renders Juba's act nearly unconscious is not clear, but the sexually charged language of the passage should not be taken to be demeaning. Rather, its ecstasy, delivered in the language of excited breathing and muffled hoofbeats, suggests a relationship between sexual pleasure and freedom that is corroborated by Bontemps's rather open depiction—for 1938—of Gabriel and Juba as lovers. More to the point, however, is the fact that the black colt Araby—the coachman Gabriel's favorite horse—is made a symbol of natural freedom from the beginning of the book. In riding Prosser's black horse in his own riding boots, Juba inverts his masculine domination, claiming command over her own body and sexuality and draining the master's potency into her own ecstatic signal of liberty.

The significance of Juba's ride is clarified if one sets it in relation to another of Bontemps's more disturbing inventions, Criddle's meditations on bloodletting and the rape of a white woman. Positioned to guard the house of a farmer located on the road to be traveled by the insurgents, so as to keep him from rousing any alarm, Criddle relishes the possible violence and compares it in his mind to hog-killing: "Criddle knew how to hush their squeals. . . . you just stuck the knife in where that big vein comes down the throat; you gave the blade a turn and it was all over." Thoughts of raping the farmer's daughter pass in and out of Criddle's mind; but though Criddle kills the farmer and neither rapes nor kills the daughter, who escapes, Bontemps's own language grotesquely magnifies the sexual implications of Criddle's penchant for violence: "He held his sword arm tense; the scythe blade rose, stiffened, stiffened and remained erect." And later: "He could feel the thing getting stiffer and stiffer in his hand." The purpose of this eroticism seems manifold. Sexual revenge, even though it was never in evidence in the major slave rebellions in the United States, might indeed appear a just form of retribution against masters who had raped their share of black women or against white women who had taken pleasure in the humiliation of black men. Like Juba's ride, moreover, Criddle's rape fantasy is circuitously connected in his mind to liberty: "She needs a big buck nigger to—no, not that. Gabriel done say too many times don't touch no womens. This here is all business this night. What that they calls it? Freedom? Yes, that's the ticket, and I reckon it feel mighty good. . . . Criddle knew what blood was like. He remembered hog-killing day."

The main question that surrounds these passages, however, concerns not what role they play in Bontemps's imagined account of the revolt from the slaves' perspective. Despite their masculinist bias, the passages add a psychological dimension that is justified by the sexual dynamics of slavery. But Bontemps wrote in the era of Jim Crow, when the sexual dynamics had changed significantly, with lynching too much a commonplace and the specious charge of rape a mask for unbridled white racial hatred. He wrote, to be more specific, in the era of Scottsboro—the "depressing subject matter" that Bontemps said provided one motive for his novel—and it is hard not to read *Black Thunder*'s deliberate, and dangerous, evocation of sexual revenge in that context. As the two scenes just cited suggest, Bontemps's reaction split into

two parts: Criddle's bloody fantasies and his "hog-killing" murder make sudden, intense violence an act of protest, the incarnation of racist sexual demonology come to life; whereas the sexualized display of Juba's ride, like her moral resistance to the whipping by Prosser, reclaims the black woman's body as her own, no longer the master's. Whether or not these scenes are equivalent, both speak to the gross miscarriage of justice in the Scottsboro case, in which the convictions for rape and assault were not simply based on questionable evidence but flouted contrary evidence. (Aside from the defense's shredding of Victoria Price's own moral character and thus her credibility before the court, examining doctors could testify to no motile sperm; no semen on her clothing; no vaginal injuries; and no significant bodily bruises or injuries to her back—this despite her claim of having been violently raped by six young men while lying barebacked in a train car of jagged gravel.) "Rape," in other words, was simply an idea; as Scottsboro and comparable cases surrounding it made clear, the mere presence of a black man in the vicinity of a white woman swearing against him was enough for conviction.

· · ·

Eventually, through the heroic defiance of entrenched racism by Judge James Horton, Supreme Court intervention, retrials, the passage of time, and parole, all of the five convicted Scottsboro defendants were released from their life sentences, the last in 1950—nineteen years too late. At the time Bontemps wrote, however, it was not clear that they would escape the death penalty, which was returned by jury after jury no matter how preposterous the evidence. Gabriel's sentence and execution therefore resonate with the likelihood that the innocent Scottsboro defendants would also die, as had many before them, under the cloak of law or not; and his testimony to the meaning of liberty stands as a repudiation of the radical decline in African-American rights since Reconstruction and the imminent execution of young men whose only crime was being black.

There is no evidence that the historical Gabriel testified at all. Although Bontemps pictures Gabriel snapping at Mingo to be silent, to "die like a free man," when Mingo is about to give information about French propaganda that influenced the conspiracy, he nonetheless creates a fairly long colloquy between Gabriel and the prosecutor that allows the black leader to articulate his own natural rights philosophy and to terrify the court by evidence of the reach and preparation of the slave rebels. The novel's Gabriel outlines no grand strategy of economic rights and subordinates all influence of political propaganda to his own argument that "a man is got a right to have his freedom in the place where he's born"—an argument as relevant to Bontemps's contemporary South as to Gabriel's Virginia. Gabriel does not confront his former master, and his testimony to the incredulous court is not so dramatic as the reply of one of the Vesey conspirators who, when later asked his intentions by his unbelieving master, replied: "To kill you, rip open your belly and throw your guts in your face." Gabriel's final testimony, aside from his repeated rumination that "maybe we should [have] paid attention to the signs," is instead calmly secure, even serene in its vision of liberty:

> "Did you imagine other well-fed, well-kept slaves would join you?"
> "Wouldn't you j'ine us, was you a slave, suh?"
> "Don't be impudent. You're still a black—"
> "I been a free man—and a gen'l, I reckon."
> "And stop saying general, too. Ringleader of mad dogs. That's what you've been.
>   I call on this court of justice—"

The rest seems babble, the "conjure" of legal language to Gabriel, who drifts into revery. Even though it does nothing to undermine the transcendent truth of Gabriel's freedom, the prosecutor's question about the allegiance of the mass of slaves is not only historically pertinent but psychologically necessary. Still, those slaves who would not join the conspiracy—a number lost to the vicissitudes of providence or chance—are immaterial compared with those who joined and then betrayed.

From the courtroom trial of Gabriel, Bontemps turns directly to the slaves' own trial, as it were, of the traitors Ben and Pharaoh. If Gabriel's punishment dignifies him, the punishment by conjure of Ben and Pharaoh demeans them. The character of Ben in *Black Thunder* is a composite of two figures: first, the actual Ben Woolfolk, whose historical role as an active participant and recruiter who turned traitor was similar to the role given him by Bontemps in the novel; and second, Tom, who along with Pharaoh was a slave belonging to Mosby Sheppard, one of Prosser's neighbors (Mosby is named Moseley in *Black Thunder*). The actual Tom and Pharaoh betrayed the conspiracy to their master the day the rebellion was to begin; Ben Woolfolk, seized outside Richmond as he prepared to spread the word of the rising to recruits elsewhere, promised information about the plot in exchange for his own pardon. Whereas some twenty-seven slaves were executed and ten more sold, Governor Monroe, following the instructions of a grateful legislature, purchased Tom and Pharaoh from Sheppard (for five hundred dollars each) and gave them their freedom. Bontemps, however, shuns such rewards, instead leaving Pharaoh and Ben at the mercy of the folk whom they have betrayed. The concluding chapters of the novel therefore view folk belief from a different perspective: the disabling fear of "stars," "signs," and "bad hands" cast against the conspiracy that Bontemps integrates into its collapse in the face of the preternatural storm ultimately becomes a mechanism of power and revenge within the community. Far from being inconsistent or arcane, however, this ambivalence in the deployment of vernacular powers accords with the role of conjure in slavery, which can only be judged from a double point of view.

By its very nature conjure stood on the margins of "belief" as that concept was normally understood by the masters and by historians of slave culture since, who in whole or part have frequently dismissed conjure as "superstition." One of the earliest ethnological essays to study conjure, by Leonora Herron and Alice Bacon in the *Southern Workman*, accurately summed up the prevailing postbellum view that conjure was "a relic of African days, though strange and incongruous growths rising from association with the white race, added to and distorted it from time to time, till it became a curious conglomerate of fetichism, divination, quackery, incantation and demonology." According to the accounts of slave culture, the conjurer, often seen to derive his or her power from African fetishistic belief, was believed to have the power to charm or curse or heal individuals. By the use of bags or balls filled with various secret ingredients (a trick, mojo, toby, hand); by using roots or animal parts made into a potion or poison, or other common items such as hair, pins, bones, cloth, feathers; by a hex or a look that could cast a spell such as a reptile infestation; by turning into a witch and riding the victim at night—by all manner of magic activities in which the aura of secret power was requisite, conjure exercised an important psychological and cultural power. Whatever ratio of actual power, chicanery, psychological suggestion, homeopathy, coincidence, or luck was involved, conjurers played significant roles within many slave communities and many African-American communities after slavery. Either alongside or in place of Christianity, African spiritualism revived in the form of conjure flourished in part as a response to the hardships of bondage and the slavemasters' deliberate stripping away of long-standing African cultural and spiritual practices. In this respect, conjure was a vehicle for the retention of African beliefs in which resistance and heroism alike were possible, as well as the formation of an African-based identity protected from the censorship of the masters.

The fact that conjure seldom worked on whites—or to put it another way, the fact that most whites did not believe in it—gave its cultural uniqueness a corresponding practical liability. Many slaves apparently believed that conjure could influence the lives of their masters and by extension their own treatment as slaves (in this regard conjurers commonly attempted to influence the forthcoming punishment of slaves, their marriages and separations, and similar events governed directly by the master's capricious will). Even so, the effects of conjure were far more often felt directly only by blacks themselves. Despite the fact that conjure posed no direct threat to the plantation regime and seldom changed the balance of power in the slaves' favor, it nevertheless formed a hidden semiotic code and system of belief that operated secretly, set apart from the white command of slaveholding. As Lawrence Levine has pointed out, belief in conjure represented the fact that whites were not necessarily omnipotent, that there were "forces they could not control, areas in which slaves could act with more knowledge and authority than their masters, ways in which the powers of the whites could be muted if not thwarted entirely." What mattered, then, was not that conjurers had any obvious power over the masters but rather that they had powers that the masters lacked or ignorantly dismissed.

This is nowhere more evident in *Black Thunder* than in the revenge taken against Ben and Pharaoh, which comes from no identifiable quarter but is implicitly identified with the world of conjure that is invoked again and again in the book as a power that Gabriel has neglected to respect and to utilize. After the conspiracy has fallen apart and Gabriel is a renegade, Juba obtains a "hand" to protect him, but he never comes to get it; the episode has no consequence. On the one hand, then, conjure seems to work contrary to the rational justifications for liberty upon which Gabriel relies; but on the other, it works to punish those who betray him. No sooner has he testified in court than Ben's relief turns to sickness:

> Suddenly in the midst of his rejoicing a kind of nausea commenced rising in Ben's stomach. Nothing from his head, mind you, nothing in his thought telling him he was a no-'count swine and lower than any dog, just something from his stomach making him so sick he wanted to vomit. He pictured his ruffled shirt-front soiled by his sickness, smeared loathsomely, and with a shiver of revulsion, he found his hand across his breast.
>
> Lordy, Jesus, I ain't being no dog. I ain't being low-down. I's just being like you made me, Marse Jesus. This here freedom and all ain't nothing to me.

Bontemps's fine study of Ben, the self-important, satisfied house servant who is pleased to be recognized as a "good boy" for his obsequious devotion to his masters, exploits the contest between African spiritualism and Christianity, which could be yoked in resistance to slavery, as in African-American worship generally, but could also split into irreconcilable opposites. Just like the savior renounced by Langston Hughes in "Goodbye, Christ," his famous 1932 poem inspired in part by Scottsboro (his 1931 poem, "Christ in Alabama," was his first response), the "Marse Jesus" called on by Ben is not the militant Christ of Mingo's liturgy, nor even the strength-giving Jesus appealed to by Stowe's Uncle Tom (who is explicitly *not* a traitor to his fellow slaves). Rather, it is the proslavery Christ beloved of the masters and ridiculed by a piercing antebellum black folk rhyme:

> White man use whip
> White man use trigger,
> But the Bible and Jesus
> Made a slave of the nigger.

Drawn into the conspiracy only by his loyalty to old Bundy, Ben envisions the rebellion as the work of the devil, a "desecrating, sinful thing" liable to slay his kindly masters and smash his comfortable plantation home: "Ben was tortured with the vision of filthy black slaves coming suddenly through those windows, pikes and cutlasses in their hands, their eyes burning with murderous passion and their feet dripping mud from the swamp. He saw the lovely hangings crash, the furniture reel and topple. . . . In another moment there were quick, choked cries of the dying, followed by wild jungle laughter." Ben's easy accommodation to the regime defined by proslavery paternalism makes Bontemps's depiction of his betrayal all the more forceful since it measures the difficulty of renouncing the "benevolent" care of slavery for the certain cataclysm of political revolt.

Ben, of course, is not simply a figure in the plot of Gabriel's story but a representative figure in the history of oppression. Whether or not Bontemps had in mind the fact that two of the Scottsboro defendants at one point attempted to offer false testimony against the others in order to secure their own pardon, he offered a searing portrait of the psychology of race betrayal. His portrait of such betrayal is comparable to that included in Sterling Brown's "Memo: For the Race Orators," which details the role traitors and spies inevitably play in a people's heritage ("This nigger too should be in history," Brown's poem begins) and singles out those who acted the part of Judas to Gabriel:

When Gabriel led his thousand on Richmond,
Armed with clubs and scythe-swords fashioned in spare
      time,
Down on the well-stocked powder-house and arsenal,
Remember Tom and Pharaoh, who blurted the news
To Mister Mosby, and sought as reward
What Gabriel wanted to fight and die for.

Ben Woolfolk is also incidentally a commentary on the passing of the "old-time Negro," a key figure in the plantation mythology in post-Reconstruction years; but as such he is also a harsh judgment on that mythology and on those slaves and their descendants who put material comfort, or the white man's Jesus, ahead of resistance and dignity. "Oh, it was hard to love freedom," says Ben in an interiorized passage that captures well the paradoxical choice between accommodation and rebellion. "It was so expensive, this love; it was such a disagreeable compulsion, such a bondage."

Like Gabriel, Ben is a figure alive in two historical moments. Yet Bontemps's invention of Ben's and Pharaoh's punishment constitutes perhaps his most telling act of historicization, for he endows conjure with mysterious powers that remain entirely free from the regime of slaveholding and rational regulation. Ascribed to unidentified slaves who seek vengeance upon Ben and Pharaoh, the conjure seems at first glance explicable either as simple attacks on the pair of traitors or as the overwrought workings of guilt. The knives that are thrown at the men out of the brush—"something as damp and cold as an icicle brushed his coat sleeve and slipped through [Ben's] hand"—make real wounds, but they come from nowhere. Pharaoh's poisoning may be actual, or it may be a result of the conjure dust on his bed and the frogs' toes in his pipe, driving him to hallucinations. The final evidence of his madness, when he vomits the coffee he believes is conjured, is deliberately ambiguous:

Then, abruptly, his shoulders rounded, he gave a little hiccough and the coffee came out of his mouth in an ugly geyser that spouted on the floor of the porch. And when he removed his hand from his eyes and saw it there, he began crying louder.

"Lordy, Ben, look at it. See there. There it is. I told you so. They fixed me. I done puked up a varmint. What is it—a snake or a lizard? Lordy! They done fixed me. Look at it there, Ben."

A common sign of conjuring, Pharaoh's inhabitation by a reptile appears as a delusion, but that hardly makes his insanity or persecution less real. Indeed, the point is that the power wielded against Pharaoh and Ben *is* psychological but at the same time external: the slave community's vengeance on those who have betrayed its leader lies in visible effects and invisible causes. "Sitting up in a tree, barking like a dog," Pharaoh is an exact inversion of the conspiracy's "mad dogs," the epithet used repeatedly to describe those slaves who could conceive such unthinkable carnage. In the scene of Pharaoh's final madness, Drucilla and the other slaves know that he has received what he deserves, and his fellow traitor Ben is left trembling for his own life and sanity, his hands growing scaly and cold, "so brittle he imagined they were like the hands of a skeleton."

The next section of *Black Thunder* begins: "An air of mystery invaded the Virginia State Legislature." Debate is about to begin, it turns out, on a bill to remove emancipated slaves from Virginia to a territory in Louisiana. The brief scene is among a number of vignettes that survey the aftermath of the failed revolt in order to demonstrate the great paranoia about slave unrest bred by the conspiracy and at the same time the absolute world of power that is quickly raised to crush all remaining threat of insurrection. Punctuated by both the spectacle and the sounds of hanging, as the convicted ringleaders of the conspiracy are periodically executed to the satisfaction of great crowds, the last chapter of

Bontemps's novel sets two arenas of power against one another—the power of the state versus the power of the slave quarters—and in the process inverts the roles of the protagonists. At critical moments Gabriel's testimony forsakes political philosophy, even language itself. But just as his song of freedom unites him to the mass of slaves he hoped to lead to freedom, it also distinguishes him from the traitors he leaves behind: "Was I a singing man, I'd sing me a song now, he thought. I'd sing me a song about lonesome, about a song-singing man long gone. No need crying about a nigger what's about to die free. I'd sing me a song, me." When the axe of Gabriel's executioner inscribes an arc and springs the trap, making his hanging rope hum like a violin string, Ben cannot get the image and sound out of his mind, nor can he "feel reassured about the knives that waited for him with the sweet brown thrashers in every hedge and clump." Gabriel, in chains and sent to the gallows, is free, while Ben, back in the paternalistic care of his good master and the regime of slavery, is condemned to a life of fear and self-incrimination, and perhaps a final judgment comparable to that of Pharaoh.

Gabriel's brief testimony in *Black Thunder*, less electric than the millenarian language of Turner's "Confessions" and devoid of the nationalist oratory a lesser novelist might have felt compelled to invent, is at once a radical intervention into the known historical record and a low-keyed replication of testimony that Gabriel might well have given. Nat Turner refused to plead guilty, and Denmark Vesey refused to speak at all; in the surviving historical record Gabriel's intentions appear only in the testimony of his followers and his betrayers. In giving Gabriel a courtroom scene, Bontemps gave back to him what the masters and history had stolen from him, a political voice with legal standing—something trial after trial ripped away from the Scottsboro defendants as well. Whereas Ben's testimony of betrayal must be vouched for by his master Sheppard to be legally credible, Gabriel tells his own tale: it does not exonerate him, but it *is* believed. Though condemned to death as a rebel, Gabriel mediates between the two worlds of power, between the political aspirations of the slaves and the betrayed revolutionary ideals of the masters, testifying to the legitimacy of both. Recoiling from the "three horrifying years," as he would later describe Alabama during the first Scottsboro trials, Bontemps may himself be said to have testified in *Black Thunder*—testified on behalf of nine young men equally betrayed by the ideals of the nation, and on behalf of all African Americans who had had little voice in claiming their natural rights and writing their own public history.

Gabriel's contemplated song of freedom, described by him as a kind of blues, recalls his own description of the conspiracy itself as a song when he says: "Well, suh, I done sung my song, I reckon. It wasn't much, though. Nothing like Toussaint. . . . [Still,] I been free. And, Lordy, I's free from now on, too." One of countless passages in *Black Thunder* rendered in an interiorized indirect discourse that belongs to the character but also serves the function of authorial narration, Gabriel's meditation toward the outset of the last chapter locates the most powerful and moving black language in the novel in thought itself. Bontemps's masterful use of indirect discourse and interior monologue is worth extended study in its own right, for it forms a second, subterranean level of black cultural life, always in contrast and resistance to the culture of the masters, as in the case of Bundy's signifying rebuke during his mortal beating at the outset of the novel: "Yes, suh, Marse Prosser, I'm taking it all. I can't prance and gallop no mo'; I'm 'bliged to take it. Yo' old sway-backed mule—that's me. Can't nobody lay it on like you, Marse Prosser." In all instances, most frequently in the case of Gabriel, the interiorized discourse is a means of creating racial consciousness—giving it a privilege

separate from the corrupt language of slaveholding law; under-
lining its subcurrent of secrecy and conspiracy against the rule
of racial domination; and making it the expression of a communal African-American culture standing centrally within the flow of
American history but lacking a publicly recognized voice.

The conceptualization of both the rebellion itself and Gabriel's
testimony as "song" elevates and heroizes both the act and its
vocal embodiment, tying each to the coded discourse of militant
resistance embedded in many of the spirituals and to the African
spiritualism inherent in the ceremonial lamentations for Bundy.
This is especially clear in the call-and-response between Bundy
and the mourners in which Gabriel himself will not participate:

> One of the moaners on the ground raised a fervent voice,
> cried in a wretched sing-song.
>
> "When Marse Prosser beat you with a stick, how you feel,
> old man?"
>
> "Feel like I wants to be free, chile."
>
> Gabriel gave the others his back, strolled to the door, rested
> one hand on the sill overhead. The chant went on.
>
> "When the jug gets low and you can't go to town, how you
> feel?"
>
> "Bound to be free, chillun, bound to be free."
>
> Gabriel left the others, walked outdoors.
>
> "When the preacher preach about Moses and the chillun,
> about David and the Philistines, how you feel, old man?"
>
> "Amen, boy. Bound to be free. You hear me? Bound to be
> free."

Bundy's funeral becomes, in effect, an exemplification of African retentions translated into Afro-Christian practice. The dying
Bundy preaches his own funeral sermon and the choral response
bears him up in a freedom song that overtly combines salvation

with the release from slavery, just as it combines the key elements of the spirituals and the blues, thereby bridging the historical gap between postcolonial Virginia and 1930s Alabama. Gabriel is abstracted from this scene so as to show his rational detachment from folk belief; but the reappearance of the trope of the freedom song in his own testimony, and in his conception of the conspiracy itself, indicates how thoroughly he has absorbed the will of the folk into his more literate political philosophy. Gabriel is musingly "thinking" again, and it is Bundy, in fact, who sees the equivalence between his song and the one Gabriel is about to sing: "I don't mind dying, but I hates to die not free. I wanted to see y'-all do something like Toussaint done. I always wanted to be free powerful bad."

Borrowing as he did from Higginson's essay on Gabriel, Bontemps would have known too that Higginson's title, "Gabriel's Defeat," was itself borrowed from a folk song that turned defeat into victory—as indeed black song has often turned defeat into victory. Not a great deal is made of the quality of Gabriel's voice— only that what it speaks, however circumscribed by the mechanisms of injustice and racism, is a sign of consciousness and freedom. Perhaps Bontemps remembered Marcus Garvey's voice, which seemed to him in the early 1920s when he heard it to be animated by a "far-off poetry, like the lyrics of some spirituals," and perhaps one might say that he looked ahead to his later documentary novel about the Fisk Jubilee Singers, *Chariot in the Sky* (1951), which placed African-American song at the heart of cultural, and hence historical, consciousness. In addition, however, the figure of "song" picks up the "talk" and "hum" of the hanging rope, thus uniting the historical incarceration and punishment of African Americans to their musical response in the spirituals and the blues, making both a primary vehicle of preserved black history.

At extremity, song gives way to pure tonality, as in the "song without words" raised by Bundy's mourners or in the frequent murmur or hum, indicated in the sound-sign "h'm," that marks black conversation in *Black Thunder*. Ranging from a simple affirmative answer to a concealing response that neither asserts nor denies (most notably, of course, when it is a reply to the master), the "h'm" also bears a kind of transcendent marking within it, not unlike the vocalization of the black preacher—as in Hurston's rendition of the Lovelace sermon—when words give way to chant and musical intonation. For example, in the conversation between Bundy and Gabriel noted above, Gabriel speaks circumspectly to Bundy of the plot: "Thinking again. It's like we been talking. You know," says Gabriel; and Bundy replies, "H'm. I was aiming to die free, me. I heard tell how in San Domingo—." Bundy's "h'm" is here linked phonetically and spiritually to the song of the communal mourners, carrying African sounds into resistance to New World slavery. But the clearest index of the ideological value embedded in the "h'm" appears in the scene where Gabriel, Ben, and the other conspirators gather on the ground of the hut to plan the rebellion: "Solomon, General John and Ditcher lay on their bellies in the hut. They were whispering with their faces near the dirt floor. Gabriel and Blue came in with Ben. No greetings, no useless words passed. The three got down and made a circle. An eery blue light pierced a crack in the wall, separated the dull silhouettes. No preliminary words, no Biblical extenuations preceded the essential plans this time." Responding to one demand that they have more weapons, Gabriel replies that they will have all they need:

> "What's mo'[,] God's going to fight them [the masters] because they oppresses the poor. Mingo read it in the Book and you heard it same as me."
> "H'm."

They all murmered. Their assent, so near the ground, seemed to rise from the earth itself. H'm. There was something warm and musical in the sound, a deep tremor. It was the earth that spoke, the fallen star.

This brief but remarkable scene yokes the fundamental strategy of indirection in slave language to a philosophy of natural rights, the murmur of the earth and the voices of the black men lying low to the ground also fusing African spiritualism with African-American political consciousness. In later oral histories, a number of slaves recalled lowering their heads or lying in holes in order to muffle the sounds of worship or talk of resistance or escape. In the case of *Black Thunder*, the conspirators' circular configuration may be both an inheritance from African sacramentalism and a strategic necessity, a syncretism of African retentions and New World pragmatism. Yet the ascription of the "h'm" to the earth itself also makes the scene a tableau of Romantic consciousness—appropriate to Gabriel's era and comparable to that which Bontemps invoked when he took the title of his fourth chapter ("A Breathing of the Common Wind") from Wordsworth's sonnet "To Toussaint L'Ouverture":

> . . . Thou hast left behind
> Powers that will work for thee; air, earth, and skies;
> There's not a breathing of the common wind
> That will forget thee: thou hast great allies;
> Thy friends are exultations, agonies,
> And love, and man's unconquerable mind.

Gabriel is an incarnation of such consciousness, his "thinking" a portrait of the unconquerable mind in search of liberation from tyranny and mastery of itself. But Bontemps's genius lay in his ability to make such consciousness simultaneously an expression of the common language of liberty in the Age of Revolution and a sign of black culture retained and transfigured in the African diaspora, which reached from Gabriel's Virginia to the Alabama of the Scottsboro boys and beyond.

"Time is not a river. Time is a pendulum," Bontemps would later write in his 1968 preface to *Black Thunder*. At that point, the recent assassination of Martin Luther King, Jr., convinced him more than ever of the veracity of his metaphor, and he feared the dream of freedom would once more be shattered as it had been in 1800. Time since has not told a clear enough tale—it has been neither pendulum nor river—but in 1938 Bontemps certainly had reason to fear that the pendulum was swinging downward. His mere association with Langston Hughes and others who had come south to write about and protest Scottsboro put his teaching job at Oakwood School in Huntsville in jeopardy. He had already researched a novel about slave rebellion by reading at Fisk University and by borrowing many books through the mail, which by itself aroused the suspicion of his employers. Before Bontemps began writing his novel, the head of his school demanded publicly that he renounce a virtually nonexistent involvement with the Scottsboro protests by burning such books in his private library as *My Bondage and My Freedom*, *The Souls of Black Folk*, and *The Autobiography of an Ex-Coloured Man*. Instead, Bontemps fled to Los Angeles and wrote *Black Thunder*. Only then, partially relieved of the nightmare, could he begin the long journey of recording and rewriting the history of black America that led him, eventually, back to the South—back, in fact, to the library at Fisk where he had first heard Gabriel's freedom song.

BIBLIOGRAPHY

In the following bibliography I have included both works cited and those that have been most influential in my interpretations, as well as studies that are among the more important in the field.

Abrahams, Roger D., ed. *Afro-American Folktales: Stories from Black Traditions in the New World*. New York: Pantheon, 1985.

——. *Deep Down in the Jungle: Negro Narrative Folklore from the Streets of Philadelphia*. Rev. ed. New York: Aldine, 1970.

Allen, William Francis, Charles Pickard Ware, and Lucy McKim. *Slave Songs of the United States*. 1867. Reprint. New York: Arno Press, 1971.

Anonymous, "Word Shadows," *Atlantic Monthly* 67 (January 1981). Reprinted in Jackson, ed., *The Negro and His Folklore*, 254–56.

Aptheker, Herbert. *American Negro Slave Revolts*. New York: International, 1943.

Armstrong, M. F., and Helen W. Ludlow. *Hampton and Its Students, with Fifty Cabin and Plantation Songs*. Arranged by Thomas P. Fenner. New York: Putnam's, 1874.

Asante, Molefi Kete. *The Afrocentric Idea*. Philadelphia: Temple University Press, 1987.

Baker, Houston A., Jr. *Blues, Ideology, and Afro-American Literature: A Vernacular Theory*. Chicago: University of Chicago Press, 1984.

——. *Modernism and the Harlem Renaissance*. Chicago: University of Chicago Press, 1987.

Berry, Mary, and John Blassingame. "Africa, Slavery, and the Roots of Contemporary Black Culture." *Massachusetts Review* 18 (1977): 501–16.

Blassingame, John W. *The Slave Community: Plantation Life in the Antebellum South*. Rev. ed. New York: Oxford University Press, 1979.

Blesh, Rudi. *Shining Trumpets: A History of Jazz*. Rev. ed. 1958. Reprint. New York: Da Capo, 1976.

Blesh, Rudi, and Harriet Janis. *They All Played Ragtime: The True Story of an American Music*. New York: Alfred A. Knopf, 1950.

Bontemps, Arna. "The Awakening: A Memoir." In *The Harlem Renaissance Remembered*, edited by Arna Bontemps. New York: Dodd, Mead, 1972.

———. *Black Thunder*. 1938. Reprint. Boston: Beacon, 1968.

———. *Chariot in the Sky*. New York: Macmillan, 1951.

———. *Drums at Dusk*. New York: Macmillan, 1939.

———. "Why I Returned." In *The Old South*, 1–25. New York: Dodd, Mead, 1973.

Borneman, Ernest. "The Roots of Jazz." In *Jazz*, edited by Nat Hentoff and Albert J. McCarthy, 1–20. New York: Holt, Rinehart and Winston, 1959.

Boskin, Joseph. *Sambo: The Rise and Demise of an American Jester*. New York: Oxford University Press, 1986.

Brown, Sterling. *Collected Poems*. Edited by Michael S. Harper. Chicago: Triquarterly, 1989.

———. "Negro Folk Expression: Spirituals, Seculars, Ballads, and Work Songs." *Phylon* 14 (Winter 1953): 45–61.

Brown, William Wells. *My Southern Home: or, the South and Its People*. 1880. Reprint. Upper Saddle River, N.J.: Gregg Press, 1968.

———. *St. Domingo: Its Revolutions and Its Patriots*. Boston: Bela Marsh, 1855.

Bruce, Dickson D., Jr. *Black Writing from the Nadir: The Evolution of a Literary Tradition, 1877–1915*. Baton Rouge: Louisiana State University Press, 1989.

Carter, Dan T. *Scottsboro: A Tragedy of the American South*. Baton Rouge: Louisiana State University Press, 1969.

Charters, Ann. *Nobody: The Story of Bert Williams*. New York: Macmillan, 1970.

Chesnutt, Helen M. *Charles Waddell Chesnutt: Pioneer of the Color Line*. Chapel Hill: University of North Carolina Press, 1952.

Chirgwin, A. M. "The Vogue of the Negro Spiritual." *Edinburgh Review* 247 (January 1928): 57–74.

Cohen, Norm. *Long Steel Rail: The Railroad in American Folksong*. Urbana: University of Illinois Press, 1981.

Cone, James H. *The Spirituals and the Blues: An Interpretation*. New York: Seabury Press, 1972.

Courlander, Harold. *Negro Folk Music, U.S.A.* New York: Columbia University Press, 1963.

Creel, Margaret Washington. *"A Peculiar People": Slave Religion and Community Culture among the Gullahs*. New York: New York University Press, 1988.

Crenshaw, Files, Jr., and Kenneth A. Miller. *Scottsboro: The Firebrand of Communism*. Montgomery, Ala.: Brown Printing, 1936.

Cuney-Hare, Maud. *Negro Musicians and Their Music*. Washington, D.C.: Associated Publishers, 1936.

Davis, Gerald L. *I Got the Word in Me and I Can Sing It You Know: A Study of the Performed African-American Sermon*. Philadelphia: University of Pennsylvania Press, 1985.

Davis, Mary Kemp. "Arna Bontemps' *Black Thunder*: The Creation of an Authoritative Text of 'Gabriel's Defeat.'" *Black American Literature Forum* 23 (Spring 1989): 17–36.

———. "From Death unto Life: The Rhetorical Function of Funeral Rites in Arna Bontemps' *Black Thunder*." *Journal of Ritual Studies* 1 (1987): 85–100.

Dett, R. Nathaniel. *Religious Folk-Songs of the Negro as Sung at Hampton Institute*. Hampton, Va.: Hampton Institute Press, 1927.

Dillard, J. L. *Black English: Its History and Usage in the United States*. New York: Random House, 1972.

Dormon, James H. "Shaping the Popular Image of Post-Reconstruction American Blacks: The 'Coon Song' Phenomenon of the Gilded Age." *American Quarterly* 40 (December 1988): 450–71.

Douglass, Frederick. *My Bondage and My Freedom*. Edited by William L. Andrews. Urbana: University of Illinois Press, 1987.

Du Bois, W. E. B. *The Souls of Black Folk*. 1903. Reprint. New York: Penguin, 1989.

Dundes, Alan, ed. *Mother Wit from the Laughing Barrel: Readings in the Interpretation of Afro-American Folklore*. 1973. Reprint. Jackson: University of Mississippi Press, 1990.

Dvorak, Antonin. "Music in America" (1895). Reprinted in Jackson, ed., *The Negro and His Folklore*, 263–73.

Egerton, Douglas R. "Gabriel's Conspiracy and the Election of 1800." *Journal of Southern History* 56 (May 1990): 191–214.

Ellison, Ralph. "The Charlie Christian Story." In *Shadow and Act*, 233–40. 1964. Reprint. New York: Vintage, 1972.

Epstein, Dena. *Sinful Tunes and Spirituals: Black Folk Music to the Civil War*. Urbana: University of Illinois Press, 1977.

Fisher, Miles Mark. *Negro Slave Songs in the United States*. 1953. Reprint. Secaucus, N.J.: Citadel Press, 1978.

Fisher, William Arms. *Seventy Negro Spirituals*. Boston: Oliver Ditson, 1926.

Franklin, C. L. *Give Me This Mountain: Life History and Selected Sermons*. Edited by Jeff Todd Titon. Urbana: University of Illinois Press, 1989.

Fullinwider, S. P. *The Mind and Mood of Black America*. Homewood, Ill.: Dorsey Press, 1969.

Gates, Henry Louis, Jr. *Figures in Black: Words, Signs, and the "Racial" Self*. New York: Oxford University Press, 1987.

————. *The Signifying Monkey: A Theory of Afro-American Literary Criticism*. New York: Oxford University Press, 1988.

Genovese, Eugene D. *From Rebellion to Revolution: Afro-American Slave Revolts in the Making of the New World*. Baton Rouge: Louisiana State University Press, 1979.

————. *Roll, Jordan, Roll: The World the Slaves Made*. New York: Random House, 1974.

Griaule, Marcel. *Conversations with Ogotemmeli: An Introduction to Dogon Religious Ideas*. London: Oxford University Press, 1965.

Handy, W. C., and Abbe Niles. *Blues: An Anthology*. 1926. Reprint. New York: Da Capo, 1990.

Harding, Vincent. *There Is a River: The Black Struggle for Freedom in America*. New York: Random House, 1981.

Hatcher, William E. *John Jasper*. New York: F. H. Revell Co., 1908.

Hazzard-Gordon, Katrina. *Jookin': The Rise of Social Dance Formations in African-American Culture*. Philadelphia: Temple University Press, 1990.

Hemenway, Robert E. *Zora Neale Hurston: A Literary Biography*. Urbana: University of Illinois Press, 1977.

Herron, Leonora, and Alice M. Bacon. "Conjuring and Conjure Doctors." *Southern Workman* 24 (1895). Reprinted in Dundes, ed., *Mother Wit from the Laughing Barrel*, 359–68.

Herskovits, Melville. *The Myth of the Negro Past*. 1941. Reprint. Boston: Beacon, 1958.

Higginson, Thomas Wentworth. *Travellers and Outlaws: Episodes in American History*. Boston: Lee and Shepard, 1889.

Hodier, Andre. *Jazz: Its Evolution and Essence*. Rev. ed. Translated by David Noakes. New York: Grove Press, 1956.

Holloway, Joseph, E., ed. *Africanisms in American Culture*. Bloomington: Indiana University Press, 1990.

Huggins, Nathan. *Harlem Renaissance*. New York: Oxford University Press, 1971.

Hunt, Alfred D. *Haiti's Influence on Antebellum America: Slumbering Volcano in the Caribbean*. Baton Rouge: Louisiana State University Press, 1988.

Hurston, Zora Neale. "Characteristics of Negro Expression," "Conversions and Visions," "Shouting," "Spirituals and Negro Spirituals," "The Sermon." In *Negro: An Anthology* edited by Nancy Cunard. 1934. Reprint. Abridged edition by Hugh Ford. New York: Frederick Ungar, 1970.

————. *Dust Tracks on a Road: An Autobiography*. 1942. Reprint. Urbana: University of Illinois Press, 1984.

————. "High John De Conquer," "The Sanctified Church." In *The Sanctified Church*. Berkeley: Turtle Island, 1981.

———. *Jonah's Gourd Vine*. 1934. Reprint. New York: Harper, 1990.

———. *Moses, Man of the Mountain*. 1939. Reprint. Urbana: University of Illinois Press, 1984.

———. *Mules and Men: Negro Folktales and Voodoo Practices in the South*. 1935. Reprint. New York: Harper, 1970.

———. *Tell My Horse: Voodoo and Life in Haiti and Jamaica*. 1938. Reprint. New York: Harper, 1990.

———. *Their Eyes Were Watching God*. 1937. Reprint. Urbana: University of Illinois Press, 1978.

Jackson, Bruce, ed. *The Negro and His Folklore in Nineteenth-Century Periodicals*. Austin: University of Texas Press, 1967.

Jahn, Janheinz. *Muntu: African Culture in the Western World*. 1958. Reprint. New York: Grove Weidenfeld, 1990.

Johnson, Barbara. "Thresholds of Difference: Structures of Address in Zora Neale Hurston." *Critical Inquiry* 12 (Autumn 1985): 278–89.

Johnson, J. Rosamond. *Rolling along in Song: A Chronological Survey of American Negro Music*. New York: Viking, 1937.

Johnson, James Weldon. *Along This Way*. 1933. Reprint. New York: Viking, 1968.

———. *The Autobiography of an Ex-Coloured Man*. 1912. Reprint. New York: Hill and Wang, 1960.

———. *Black Manhattan*. 1930. Reprint. New York: Atheneum, 1972.

———. *The Book of American Negro Poetry*. 1922. Reprint. New York: Harcourt, Brace and World, 1969.

———. "The Dilemma of the Negro Author." *American Mercury* 15 (December 1928): 477–81.

———. *God's Trombones: Seven Negro Sermons in Verse*. 1927. Reprint. New York: Penguin, 1976. Recording of Johnson's reading of selections from *God's Trombones*, Yale University Library, Division of Historical Sound Recordings.

———. *Saint Peter Relates an Incident: Selected Poems*. New York: Viking, 1935.

Johnson, James Weldon, and J. Rosamond Johnson. *Books of American Negro Spirituals*. 1925, 1926. 2 vols. in 1. Reprint. New York: Da Capo, 1969.

Jones, Leroi. *Blues People: Negro Music in White America*. New York: William Morrow, 1963.

Jordan, Winthrop D. *White over Black: American Attitudes toward the Negro, 1550–1812*. 1968. Reprint. New York: Norton, 1977.

Joyner, Charles. *Down by the Riverside: A South Carolina Slave Community*. Urbana: University of Illinois Press, 1984.

Kennedy, R. Emmett. *Mellows: A Chronicle of Unknown Singers*. New York: Albert and Charles Boni, 1925.

Kochman, Thomas, ed. *Rappin' and Stylin' Out: Communication in Urban Black America*. Chicago: University of Illinois Press, 1972.

Krehbiel, Henry Edward. *Afro-American Folksongs: A Study in Racial and National Music*. 1914. Reprint. New York: Frederick Ungar, 1962.

Levine, Lawrence. *Black Culture and Black Consciousness: Afro-American Folk Thought from Slavery to Freedom*. New York: Oxford University Press, 1977.

Levy, Eugene. *James Weldon Johnson: Black Leader, Black Voice*. Chicago: University of Chicago Press, 1973.

Locke, Alain. "The Negro Spirituals." In *The New Negro*, edited by Alain Locke, 199–213. 1925. Reprint. New York: Atheneum, 1974.

Logan, Rayford W. *The Betrayal of the Negro: From Rutherford B. Hayes to Woodrow Wilson*. 1954. Reprint. New York: Collier Books, 1965.

Lomax, John A., and Alan Lomax, *American Ballads and Folk Songs*. New York: Macmillan, 1934.

Lovell, John, Jr. *Black Song: The Forge and the Flame. The Story of How the Afro-American Spiritual Was Hammered Out*. New York: Macmillan, 1972.

Marsh, J. B. T. *The Story of the Jubilee Singers; With Their Songs*. Boston: Houghton, Mifflin, 1880.

McPherson, James A. *Railroad: Trains and Train People in American Culture*. New York: Random House, 1976.

Mellers, Wilfrid. *Music in a New Found Land*. New York: Alfred A. Knopf, 1964.

Mitchell, Henry H. *Black Preaching*. Philadelphia: Lippincott, 1970.

Mitchell-Kernan, Claudia. "Signifying, Loud-Talking, and Marking." In Kochman, ed. *Rappin' and Stylin' Out*, 315–35.

Mullin, Gerald W. *Flight and Rebellion: Slave Resistance in Eighteenth-Century Virginia*. New York: Oxford University Press, 1972.

Murphy, Jeanette Robinson. "The Survival of African Music in America." *Popular Science Monthly* 55 (1899). Reprinted in Jackson, ed., *The Negro and His Folklore*, 327–39.

Murray, Albert. *Stomping the Blues*. New York: Da Capo, 1976.

Nash, Gary B. *Race and Revolution*. Madison, Wis.: Madison House, 1990.

Odum, Howard W., and Guy B. Johnson. *The Negro and His Songs: A Study of Typical Negro Songs in the South*. Chapel Hill: University of North Carolina Press, 1925.

——— . *Negro Workaday Songs*. Chapel Hill: University of North Carolina Press, 1926.

Oliver, Paul. *Blues Fell This Morning: Meaning in the Blues*. London: Cambridge University Press, 1960.

——— . *Savannah Syncopators: African Retentions in the Blues*. New York: Stein and Day, 1970.

——— . *Songsters and Saints: Vocal Traditions on Race Records*. New York: Cambridge University Press, 1984. Accompanying long-playing records, *Songsters and Saints*, issued by Matchbox Records.

——— . *The Story of the Blues*. Philadelphia: Chilton Book, 1969.

Ostendorf, Berndt. *Black Literature in White America*. Totowa, N.J.: Barnes and Noble, 1982.

Owsley, Frank. "Scottsboro, the Third Crusade; The Sequel to Abolitionism and Reconstruction." *American Review* 1 (June 1933): 257–85.

Park, Robert E. *Race and Culture*. 1918. Reprint. Glencoe, Ill.: Free Press, 1950.

Parrish, Lydia. *Slave Songs of the Georgia Sea Islands*. 1942. Reprint. Athens: University of Georgia Press, 1992.

Peabody, Charles S. "Notes on Negro Music." *Journal of American Folklore* 16 (1903): 148–52.

Peek, Philip M. "The Power of Words in African Verbal Arts." *Journal of American Folklore* 94 (1981): 19–43.

Pelton, Robert D. *The Trickster in West Africa: A Study of Mythic Irony and Sacred Delight*. Berkeley: University of California Press, 1980.

Philips, Ulrich B. *Life and Labor in the Old South*. 1929. Reprint. Boston: Little, Brown, 1963.

Pipes, William H. *Say Amen, Brother: Old-Time Negro Preaching*. New York: William-Frederick, 1951.

Puckett, Newbell Niles. *Folk Beliefs of the Southern Negro*. 1926. Reprint. Montclair, N.J.: Patterson Smith, 1968.

Raboteau, Albert J. *Slave Religion: The "Invisible Institution" in the Antebellum South*. New York: Oxford University Press, 1978.

Ramsey, Frederic, Jr. *Been Here and Gone*. New Brunswick: Rutgers University Press, 1960.

Rathbun, F. G. "The Negro Music of the South," *Southern Workman* 22 (November 1893): 174.

Rawick, George P. *From Sundown to Sunup: The Making of the Black Community*. Westport, Conn.: Greenwood Press, 1972.

Roberts, John W. *From Trickster to Badman: The Black Folk Hero in Slavery and Freedom*. Philadelphia: University of Pennsylvania Press, 1989.

Rosenberg, Bruce A. *Can These Bones Live? The Art of the American Folk Preacher*. 1970. Rev. ed. Urbana: University of Illinois Press, 1988.

Sargeant, Winthrop. *Jazz: Hot and Hybrid*. 3d ed. 1946. Reprint. New York: Da Capo Press, 1975.

Scarborough, Dorothy. *On the Trail of Negro Folk-Songs*. Cambridge: Harvard University Press, 1925.

Schafer, William J., and Johannes Riedel, *The Art of Ragtime: Form and Meaning of an Original Black American Art*. 1973. Reprint. New York: Da Capo Press, 1977.

Schuller, Gunther. *Early Jazz: Its Roots and Musical Development*. New York: Oxford University Press, 1968.

Sidran, Ben. *Black Talk*. 1971. Reprint. New York: Da Capo, 1983.

Skerrett, Joseph T., Jr. "Irony and Symbolic Action in James Weldon Johnson's *The Autobiography of an Ex-Coloured Man*." *American Quarterly* 32 (Winter 1980): 540–58.

Smitherman, Geneva. *Talkin' and Testifyin': The Language of Black America*. Detroit: Wayne State University Press, 1986.

Sobel, Mechal. *Trabelin' On: The Slave Journey to an Afro-Baptist Faith*. Westport, Conn.: Greenwood Press, 1979.

Southern, Eileen. *The Music of Black Americans: A History*. New York: Norton, 1971.

Spencer, Jon Michael. *Sacred Symphony: The Chanted Sermon of the Black Preacher*. New York: Greenwood Press, 1987.

Spillers, Hortense. "Moving On Down the Line." *American Quarterly* 40 (March 1988): 83–108.

Starobin, Robert S., ed. *Denmark Vesey: The Slave Conspiracy of 1822*. Englewood Cliffs, N.J.: Prentice-Hall, 1970.

Stearns, Marshall, and Jean Stearns. *Jazz Dance: The Story of American Vernacular Dance*. London: Macmillan, 1966.

———. *The Story of Jazz*. New York: Oxford University Press, 1958.

Stepto, Robert B. *From behind the Veil: A Study of Afro-American Narrative*. (Urbana: University of Illinois Press, 1979.

———. "Zora Neale Hurston and the Lovelace Sermon: Issues of Authorship in Vernacular Culture" (unpublished essay).

Stoller, Paul. "Sound in Songhay Cultural Experience." *American Ethnologist* (1984): 559–70.

Stone, Albert E. *The Return of Nat Turner: History, Literature, and Cultural Politics in Sixties America*. Athens: University of Georgia Press, 1991.

Stuckey, Sterling. *Slave Culture: Nationalist Theory and the Foundations of Black America*. New York: Oxford University Press, 1987.

Sundquist, Eric J. *To Wake the Nations: Race in the Making of American Literature*. Cambridge: Harvard University Press, 1993.

Taylor, Clyde. " 'Salt Peanuts': Sound and Sense in African / American Oral / Musical Creativity." *Callaloo* 5 (October 1982): 1–11.

Thomas, H. Nigel. *From Folklore to Fiction: A Study of Folk Heroes and Rituals in the Black American Novel*. New York: Greenwood Press, 1988.

Toll, Robert C. *Blacking Up: The Minstrel Show in Nineteenth-Century America*. New York: Oxford University Press, 1974.

Toll, William. *The Resurgence of Race: Black Social Theory from Reconstruction to the Pan-African Conferences*. Philadelphia: Temple University Press, 1979.

Van Vechten, Carl. "Folksongs of the American Negro." In *"Keep A-Inchin' Along": Selected Writings of Carl Van Vechten about Black Art and Letters*. Edited by Bruce Kellner. Westport, Conn.: Greenwood Press, 1979.

Wagner, Jean. *Black Poets of the United States*. Translated by Kenneth Douglas. 1962. Reprint. Urbana: University of Illinois Press, 1973.

Waldo, Terry. *This Is Ragtime*. New York: Hawthorne Books, 1976.

Walker, George W. "The Real 'Coon' on the American Stage." *Theatre Magazine* 6 (August 1906): 224–26.

Wall, Cheryl A. "Zora Neale Hurston: Changing Her Own Words." In *American Novelists Revisited: Essays in Feminist Criticism*, edited by Fritz Fleischmann, 371–93. Boston: G. K. Hall, 1982.

Weil, Dorothy. "Folklore Motifs in Arna Bontemps' *Black Thunder*." *Southern Folklore Quarterly* 35 (March 1971): 1–14.

White, Newman A. *American Negro Folk-Songs*. Cambridge: Harvard University Press, 1928.

Wilgus, D. K. "The Negro-White Spiritual." In Dundes, ed. *Mother Wit from the Laughing Barrel*, 81–94.

Williamson, Joel. *The Crucible of Race: Black-White Relations in the American South since Emancipation*. New York: Oxford University Press, 1984.

————. *New People: Miscegenation and Mulattoes in the United States*. New York: Free Press, 1980.

Wilmore, Gayraud S. *Black Religion and Black Radicalism: An Interpretation of the Religious History of Afro-American People*. Rev. ed. Maryknoll, N.Y.: Orbis Books, 1983.

Wittke, Carl. *Tambo and Bones: A History of the American Minstrel Stage*. Durham, N.C.: Duke University Press, 1930.

Woll, Allen, *Black Musical Theatre: From Coontown to Dreamgirls*. Baton Rouge: Louisiana State University Press, 1989.

Work, John W. *American Negro Songs and Spirituals*. New York: Bonanza Books, 1940.

Young, James O. *Black Writers of the Thirties*. Baton Rouge: Louisiana State University Press, 1973.

INDEX